TABLE OF CONTENTS

CHAPTER 1 Africans, Cotton, and America -1

CHAPTER 2 The *Other* Side of Freedom-28

CHAPTER 3 Inferiority Is Complex-70

CHAPTER 4 A Way Out-102

CHAPTER 5 Blurry Separation Lines-107

CHAPTER 6 A New Normal-126

CHAPTER 7 American: Not *Also* American-152

CHAPTER 8 Pop Culture-186

CHAPTER 9 Voting Rights....and Wrongs-222

CHAPTER 10 A New Song-232

CHAPTER 11 Prepped to Accept-254

CHAPTER 12 The Evolution of Media-265

CHAPTER 13 *The* President-297

CHAPTER 14 Why I *Hate* Black History Month-308

CHAPTER 15 A Farewell to WelfARE-323

CHAPTER 16 She Loves Me Not-330

CHAPTER 1

Africans, Cotton, and America

The first Africans were brought to America to be used as slave labor, by former Britons, who all but annihilated the native population and established themselves as *Americans*. More specifically, the Africans were brought here to pick cotton. Around the time America gained its *independence* from Britain, cotton was very much in demand throughout the world. Used, mostly, for making clothes. And the American south was fertile and perfect for growing it.

The only problem was, they needed bodies to pick it. Bodies who could handle working in the hot sun all day. So that is why their attention turned to the African continent. These new European Americans first tried using other White people to pick cotton, which resulted in disaster. They then tried the Native Americans who also couldn't stand the extended periods of time working in the hot sun, picking cotton, *and* because they *refused* to do so.

Having the opportunity for a bright future in the cotton trade at stake, they decided to forcefully bring Africans to this country, for the sole purpose of providing free labor, mostly, for their cotton industry. Although slavery wasn't limited to the southern states, as assumed by many.

The Middle Passage is the term used to describe the stretch of the Atlantic Ocean which reaches from the western coast of the African continent to the eastern coast of the North American continent and eastern coast of the South American continent. This was the route traveled by the slave traders, or "slavers", as they were often referred to.

These were the ships and crew who transported Africans from their own continent to the Americas to be used as slave labor. For the purpose of expediency, most of the Africans were taken from the regions located on the western coast of Africa. Such as countries now known as Nigeria, Ghana, and Senegal.

The practice of Africans capturing, and enslaving people of rival tribes is something that is known about in African history. Also, many of the slaves who wound up on ships bound for America, were sold to the slave traders by their fellow Africans. Who after discovering the cruel and inhumane treatment that the expatriated Africans received *on the way to* and *after reaching America*, are said to have regretted it.

There is no proof to bear this out, but some White Americans are fond of pointing to the fact that our ancestors were sold to *their* ancestors to use as slaves, by other Africans. That doesn't excuse the way Africans were treated under the despicable institution of *American* slavery.

Accounts of the conditions under which these Africans were transported vary from one historian to another, but the one thing that they agree on, is that they were forced to make the journey under deplorable conditions. Many were lost to death from diseases which spread quickly because of living in darkness, their own waste, and being chained together in such close quarters. Sometimes being chained to the floor of the ship (which was the norm) next to a dead body, for days. These Africans were looked upon as *sub-human cargo* and not as people, at all.

Rather than living under these circumstances, many of the Africans chose to commit suicide, by jumping into the ocean and by other means. Sometimes they would refuse to eat and succeed at suicide that way. At other times they would be force-fed to keep them alive. Their only value to their captors was commercial, but that was the bottom line anyway, keeping them alive until their arrival at their destinations.

The slave trade was heavily invested in by banks, insurance companies, universities, and other businesses, some of whom are still around today. The gain of profit was placed above the human condition, when it came to the slaves.

Transporting slave "cargo" as they were referred to, was so despicable that the sailors detested the job and only signed on when they couldn't get any other work.

Countries who took part in the slave trade were England, Spain, France, Portugal, Denmark, Norway, the Netherlands, Sweden, and Brandenburg, which is now called Germany. A large percentage of Africans died in route to their perspective new lands in America, Brazil, and the Caribbean islands.

Beginning in 1440, the slave trade carried on for the next 400 years. During the first 200 years, the transporting of Africans to the western hemisphere was dominated by the Portuguese. Most of *those* Africans ended up in what is now called Brazil. After that time the English began to dominate the slave trade. The journey through the middle passage could take anywhere from 1 to 6 months to complete.

The first Africans must have been terrified by the culture shock, as well as the treatment, that they received at the hands of the European slave owners after arriving here in America.

They were castigated, some were *castrated*, raped and robbed of any semblance of life as they had known it. Forbidden to speak their own languages and even to play their drums, for fear of sending messages that could lead to rebellion by those other Africans who might understand a message transmitted by drumming.

As a way of showing servitude the slaves were forced to call the slaveowner "master" or "massa" as most Africans pronounced it. Fear and intimidation were the order of the day. It was a miserable life for the slave *and* the slaveowner. The intimidation was used to keep the slaves on their toes, but the *fear* was shared by both parties. I imagine that the individual or individuals responsible for "keeping the slaves in line" didn't sleep very well.

Often, that job would be assigned to another African, under the title of overseer. The overseer had the authority to administer the whip to "unruly" slaves, when instructed to do so, by the slave owner. Naturally, the slaves hated the overseer, as much, or more, than they hated the slave owner.

The overseer would go to almost any length to prove his loyalty to his "massa", for the privilege of being treated a little better than the rest of the slaves. However, never really gaining his trust. If any slave was able to figure out an escape, the responsibility and blame would be placed squarely on the overseer's back. And most often, literally. With a whip laid to his back, if not killed.

Sometimes the overseer was a poor White man, *slightly better off* than the slaves, economically, but feeling far superior because of belonging to the White race. This allowed him the feeling of being somewhat of a slave owner himself. Their frustrations of being on the lower economic level were often taken out on the slaves. This is similar to how some poverty-stricken Whites of today often voice the opinion that Blacks *taking jobs away from them* are the reasons for their lack of jobs and opportunity.

It was *never intended* for the Africans to be a part of the social fabric of America. That is one of the main reasons why the disparities between Blacks and Whites exist until the present time. What do you do with millions of people whom you can no longer exploit, but whom are still around, and growing in numbers? And to top it off, you claim to be a democratic country whereby *all* of your citizens are created equal and liberty and justice are the rights of every single person born within your borders.

The Following is an article uncovering the fact that slavery wasn't only confined to the southern states.

The Source of the article: https://www.history.com/news

UPDATED:
FEB 5, 2019
ORIGINAL:
JUN 25, 2014

Deeper Roots of Northern Slavery Unearthed

An investigation has revealed that one of Colonial New England's most aristocratic families participated in the slave trade.

(WRITER) CHRISTOPHER KLEIN

Although often associated with the South, slavery was part of Colonial life in the North as well. Northern merchants profited from the transatlantic triangle trade of molasses, rum and slaves, and at one point in Colonial America more than 40,000 slaves toiled in bondage in the port cities and on the small farms of the North. In 1740, one-fifth of New York City's population was enslaved.

Northern slavery, though, faded in the wake of the American Revolution. By 1804, all of the Northern states had passed legislation to abolish slavery, although some of these measures were gradual. For instance, a Connecticut law passed in 1784 declared that children of enslaved African-Americans born in the future would be freed—but only after turning 25. The 1840 Census showed 17 African-Americans still enslaved in Connecticut.

A 2002 investigation by the Courant into Connecticut's involvement in slavery found that there were more than 1,100 documented voyages of slave ships from New England. While most slaves were transported to the Caribbean, some were brought back to New England. The Courant estimated that at one point there were more than 5,000 African-American slaves in Colonial Connecticut.

- **End of Article**

So, since slavery was *mostly* confined to the southern states that was where the majority of Black people lived. Before *and* after slavery. They were *confined* there *during* slavery, for obvious reasons, and *afterwards*, because they had nowhere to go, only knew the ways of the south, and most had no means by which to travel. Relocating was too difficult, and next to impossible, under the circumstances. Add to that, having no way of supporting themselves *and that* compounded with the inability to read and write. Every journey requires directions, which is most often, in the form of writing.

Because it is the gateway to knowledge, reading was forbidden for the Africans, in order to keep them ignorant, since *knowledge,* itself, is the path to freedom. A person who can read and comprehend is capable of achieving many things that an illiterate person might not even be *aware* of. It doesn't necessarily mean that the one is bright and the other one isn't. It could mean that one has had *access* to knowledge, through knowing how to read. And the other one can't read, because of not having been exposed to the tools which are necessary for *learning* to read.

For a Black person in America, during the time of slavery, learning to read the English language was punishable by blinding, and even death. That was one of the White slave owners' ways of keeping them in bondage.

Even if you decided to run away, and couldn't read, you'd have to rely on the help of someone who could. Which most often resulted in being taken back to the slave owner and punished or killed. Depending on how much you were worth to them.

To their credit, some Whites secretly taught Blacks to read and write. Under the threat of being harmed themselves, if they were even *suspected* of doing so. This would usually be a White woman teaching a Black woman. The opportunities arose because of them being more closely associated, through housekeeping, tending to the children, cooking, and, *being women*, having a more sympathetic heart, in general. In some strange way, White wives of slave owners and their Black female attendants often, secretly, had close relationships.

The wives were, most often aware that their husbands were carrying on, sexually, with whomever they chose to from the female slave population. Sometimes too ashamed or afraid to talk to other White women about their " problem", they talked about it to their Black female attendants. Leaning on one another for support. Sometimes the husbands would try to use their wives to gather information about what the slaves might be up to. Depending on how she felt, she might *help* him, or sometimes *betray* him by passing information to the slaves. Such as who was about to be sold.

One of the most hurtful tactics used during slavery was the separation of families. This was done for various reasons. Sometimes as a punishment for the one being sold. Maybe for not following orders and not being submissive enough to those in charge. At other times it might be to deprive the remaining family members of the strength of the one being sold, so as to break the bond of kinship and unity, in order to keep them weak and dependent only upon the plantation owner.

The practice of selling off various members of the same family was employed often. If a family was kept together it was usually because the plantation owner felt that it was beneficial in getting the maximum production from the *family unit*. In other words, a family who worked so hard that it would be foolish to separate them and risk a lesser output. Making the most money possible was always the objective.

Another reason for selling or trading slaves could also be for the purpose of "breeding" male and female slaves who could produce large numbers of offspring. A certain male who was known to have fathered a large number of children paired with a particular female who was also known to be fertile was often thought to be the ideal situation.

12

If a male slave, quite often referred to as a "Buck", became respected or looked up to by the rest of the slave population, he would usually have to be "broken" or sold to a plantation owner so far away that there would be no way of staying in touch with the people who looked up to him. There was another way that was referred to as, "breaking the buck."

The Black man would be stripped naked and tied, face down, to stakes by each arm and leg. All of the females of his family and everyone else would be forced to watch as the plantation owner, and sometimes his friends from other plantations, would sodomize (anally rape) the victim. This was meant to take his manhood and leave him without dignity in the eyes of his family and the other slaves.

There was always the need for maximum production. The slaves often referred to their working hours as, "From can't see to can't see." This meant working from the darkness of morning, before the sun came up. Until the darkness of evening, after the sun had gone down.

As soon as a child was able to understand how to fill a cotton sack, he or she was sent to the fields to pick cotton. Life, as African Americans knew it, was only an existence. Maximum work, minimum sleep, and not enough to eat, was the routine of a slave.

You had no jurisdiction over your own family. Your wife could be taken out of your bed to be bedded by the plantation owner anytime he desired to do so. Your children could be thrashed or raped by him and there was nothing that you could say or do about it. The living conditions were deplorable, beyond imagination.

For those wondering why African Americans would eat the parts of the pig that some of them still do (feet, intestines, testicles, brains, snout). It's customary. A carry over from our slave past when the slaveowner would take the better parts of the hog and give us the cast offs. Being inventive as we were, we would take the scraps and make them work as food for us. Such was the life of bondage. You took what you had and survived. Today some of those same castoff foods are known as, "soul food", and sought out by many people as delicacies. White people included.

To those who might wonder why there are some White people who seem to hate Black people "for nothing". Let me offer a few reasons. Some still wish for that same type of control over us and can't get over the fact that Black people are no longer their "property." Some are angry to be reminded of such a barbaric history on the part of their ancestors. Others just wish that they could make us disappear.

But for us to just disappear would mean that we would not be able to share in the fruits of our labor. The blood sweat and tears of our ancestors gave us stock in this corporation called America. Our freedom is a down payment on the compensation that *they* never received for their service in the building of this country. I only wish that I could speak to the hearts of the young people, of all races in America, to inform them of the price which has been paid by the disenfranchised of this country. To let them know that price was not cheap and deserves their best effort to make the past count towards a better America for everyone.

When you're controlling people through bondage, intimidation, and brutality, you sleep lightly and expect them to be planning ways to gain their freedom, at any time. For this reason, *both* parties are in bondage. The slave *and* the slave owner. The later because of the need to know if there is a rebellion being plotted. Is my family in danger? Which ones, if any of them, can I trust? Am I too soft on them? Am I too *hard* on them? With the slaves having many of their own concerns. Will I be sold away from my family? How do I avoid getting beaten? How can I escape? If I do, what will happen to the others?

Being illiterate kept the so-called Negro at an added disadvantage, of which they were constantly aware. Being called ignorant for not knowing, and at the same time, not *allowed* to learn. Needless to say, this must have been one of the main objectives on the minds of Black people. *Learning to read*. Especially after their emancipation. Even then, they had to keep such things as learning to read, under secrecy, for fear of appearing "uppity". A term meaning, a level of thinking that was too "high-minded" for the so-called Negro.

Since the inception of this nation, it has been filled with contradictions. "The land of the free", "All men are created equal", are some of the most obvious ones. The founding fathers by-passed some of the controversy in this, by labeling Africans as "sub- human". But they founded the country on the premise, "In God We Trust", while enslaving another human being is in direct conflict with the ways of God, according to The Holy Bible.

Some African Americans, to this day, refuse to be involved with Christianity because of the ways in which the slave owners used the Bible, falsely teaching that the Bible said the slave was meant to be subjugated and controlled by the slaveholders. And that the slave was to obey their owners at all times.

Distorting the Scriptures to suit whatever purpose they needed them for. Even telling the Africans that they were created darker than the Europeans because God had punished them that way.

To this day you can still hear some people say that because of Ham looking upon his father's nakedness, (Genesis 9:20-27) God turned *his* descendants darker than the other races, as a mark of shame. This is a misinterpretation of what is written. People with any knowledge of the true concept of slavery, especially American slavery, know that it was doomed to fail, for various reasons, from the very beginning. One reason is the sheer numbers of Africans brought to North America, which was established, by laws, as a democratic society.

There was no way possible to have a true democracy and be a slave colony at the same time. Eventually, the disenfranchised are going to want to be included. Although that struggle for inclusion carries on 'til this day. The Africans, who are now called African Americans, are still looking to gain their recognition as citizens, and not just *second-class* citizens.

The White establishment is quite unrelenting in giving up the complete package of citizenship to African Americans. And what could be accomplished with fear and intimidation in the past, is now implemented by way of subtle gestures, that are so hard to prove, that they can be thought of, *and dismissed*, as a "figment of our imaginations" by those looking from outside of the situation.

As the struggle for *real freedom* intensifies, so does the effort to keep African Americans in their "place." Making it obvious to some *non-Blacks* who never understood it before, that the grievances being put forward by African Americans are more than just complaining. The evidence is becoming more obvious that Black people are not just whining and complaining "for nothing."

A more heavy-handed style of policing is one of the most apparent areas of proof to that point. Many police officers have openly begun to treat African Americans with such disrespect and disdain, that people, of *different* races have begun to lose respect for the office of policing because of what they are witnessing.

Ever since the abolishment of slavery, the *proponents* of slavery have looked for ways to keep the memory of slavery alive. I suspect that some of them even think that slavery will return to being. Never-the-less, they hold on to their symbolisms and when questioned about it, call it pride in their heritage. To be proud of a heritage which descended from being the purveyors of slavery and *seeing that* as honorable and chivalrous is beyond my scope of understanding. The *merits* of which, are without foundation.

At the same time, I find the statement made by some African Americans, "Back in Africa we were kings and queens," as also baseless. Sure, history tells us that there were African kings and queens. But it would be foolish to believe that we were *all* kings and queens. Even if we had been, we were robbed of *whatever we were* and it's time to re-establish ourselves.

In honesty though, I understand both sides. I understand the southerner who is looking to find some "royalty" in forefathers who lived a life of grandeur and wealth in colossal mansions. But I don't understand being proud of *how they financed* that lifestyle.

I also understand the African American statement. It's saying, "We're somebody too. We were not just *born* slaves." To that I say, if you really believe that you descended from kings and queens, then begin to *carry* yourselves as kings and queens.

As African Americans, our past is part of our history and deserves to be remembered, but our present and future are much more important. We should be trying to build a legacy as a people who not only survived, but also thrived and achieved. Instead, too many of us have adopted the attitude that we can, "Only do what *they* allow us to do." There is not a lot of freedom in that way of thinking. In a sense we *are putting the chains on ourselves* when we accept that type of thinking.

If there is anything good to emerge from slavery, it must be shared by all parties, the oppressor and the oppressed. The exclusion of either party will doom the whole thing for failure. Within the history of America, since the very beginning, there has been more emphasis placed on segregation, than on education. The power structure in this country is more concerned with making, and keeping, America a White country than having it be a strong unified one. To call that ignorance would be denying the truth, because it is calculated and institutionalized bigotry. It is being done purposely.

To say that freedom for Black people in America is beginning to look like an impossible dream, is an honest summation of the facts, as they stand. We must contest for everything that is grudgingly relinquished to us. We are seldom treated with the same respect afforded our White counterparts. In fact, many White Americans don't even consider us *to be* their counterparts. That would be putting us on equal footing with them. To use a timeworn cliché, Black people are the "Last hired and the first fired," in America. To be *completely* honest, Black people are not treated with respect and equality *anywhere in the world*, outside of predominately Black countries. And even in those *Black countries*, treatment of *poor* people is often questionable.

It's no wonder Dr. King said, "I have a dream." We have been "dreaming" of better opportunities and treatment since we arrived on these shores some 400 years ago. It has been a strange existence for all parties involved. Who can relax when there is so much turmoil going on around and inside of us? We, the citizens of this great country are losing out on so much unfulfilled promise and potential. Whatever greatness we've attained as a country could be much greater if we ever truly came together as people.

We (African Americans) get glimpses of what life *could* be like when we see a beautiful property for rent or sale, only to have the price raised to ridiculous levels when it is realized that it is wanted by an African American. Not all the time, *but much too often.*

Finally, being able to get a homeowner loan, then discovering too late, because of inexperience, that the loan is a trap and you will have to default on paying it back. All because it was set up to intentionally fail from the beginning.

Having laws passed on your behalf, then watching them being rescinded. Learning about how to invest in something only to have the rules change once it's realized that *you're* involved. I once heard a man say that the stock market was made to be complicated so regular people wouldn't be able to understand it. That applies to many things that have to do with the upper echelon.

Songs have been written. Movies have been made and speeches have been recited about how to approach the pursuit of true happiness in the United States of America. The blueprint has been drawn up many times over. The real problem is that the system which is firmly in control in this country has no intention of allowing that blueprint to be implemented. Ever. Our only hope is in the fact that we still have somewhat of a democracy left. Even *that* appears to be fading quickly.

An educated society works against the level of control that the system desires to have over the common people. *Of all races*. They feed poor Whites the dream of a rich and authoritative White society. When the truth is, they're pursuing an "elitist only" White society. And we already know that not everyone can be rich. In essence, what they are saying is, "Help us to get this done and you can then be one of us." But there is a caste system at work in America just as intricate as the one in India. Think about this, Black people didn't coin the phrase, "trailer trash." Other *White* people came up with that.

I notice Black people using the phrase, "That is so ghetto", a derogatory phrase also invented by White people to describe any kind of conduct which they consider to be acting "Black." Can you see the irony in an African American taking a term that was meant to put them down and using it against themselves?

An effective method of deception is to let someone think that you're *teaching* them while feeding them false information and having them *believe* that it's true. When someone else tries to tell them what you're up to, you just say, "Oh they are lying and just don't want you knowing the truth."

Keeping people illiterate and ignorant plays a big part in the degree to which you can manipulate them. Because they have nothing to base their own opinions on, it allows you to control them by the opinions that you *give* them. Because they don't read or dig deeper for true knowledge, *your opinion* becomes *their "knowledge"*. And depending on how much loyalty they have to you, they will defend your right to do, or say, almost anything. Does this sound familiar?

Americans are loaded with opinions. Any subject that you can think of, the average American has an opinion on it. That would seem to insinuate that, mostly America is a literate and informed society. Wrong. The reality is, that we, as Americans, are being fed the opinions that our leaders *want* us to have, without telling us that is the case. If they told us we were being led, would we follow them? Most of us, probably not.

Even if a person is an avid reader, the intellect that they gain from it, still depends on *what* they read. Information is placed in strategic places in order to reach its intended audience. This is why we must be selective in what we allow to reside in our minds, knowing the difference between propaganda and truth. We have been so *successfully programmed*, as citizens of this country that most of us have no idea that this statement itself, could be even remotely true. "You must be crazy. I heard it on the news. Plus, I read it in the magazines!" Sure, you did! It was placed where you couldn't miss it.

There is an approach that is used quite frequently. When someone is fortunate enough to somehow rise to the forefront of the American society, they are sometimes welcomed into the "front hallway" of the elite. Not completely into the establishment, but just far enough in, to make them feel like they are welcome there.

After this feeling, of having arrived, has had the chance to sink in, they are then asked to perform some type of duty for their new "friends" in situations where the friends themselves are just not *trusted or believed*. Feeling privileged to have such an honor bestowed upon them, the "newcomer" is more than happy to do it. Now they have crossed over to the other side and allowed themselves to be used against the same people whom they once shared a common struggle with. Sometimes they are aware of what is taking place and sometimes they're not.

Some people are of the opinion that reading is a waste of time and isn't going to add anything to their lives. That is one of the dumbest things that I have ever heard. While just the opposite is true. Without reading, a person is left out of so many things that could be beneficial to their lives. And a person who *can read*, *but doesn't*, really makes me scratch my head in bewilderment.

Reading is pertinent to so many things. Voting, for instance, cannot be *properly* performed by an illiterate person. Ironically, many Black people have been killed for trying to learn to read *and* for trying to gain the right to vote. So, these are two things that should be high on the agenda of African Americans. Reading and voting. Because it is our right, but mostly for the fact that, reading and voting can help tremendously in changing our lives for the better.

Many years ago, I expressed to a friend that I desired to learn to read music. He replied to me that if it were him, he would rather learn to write music. The lesson wasn't lost on me because I did learn to write music, but only after I had learned to *read it first*. What he was saying to me is, don't just stop at enjoying what others have done, do something yourself, so they can have a chance to enjoy your work, as well. For that to happen, a standard has to be set.

My high school English teacher, Mrs. Mims, asked me one day, "McGee, have you ever thought about a career in writing?" Until then, I had not. Although, after that, it was there in the back of my head, I didn't give it *serious* thought until many years later. After I had learned to write songs. Then one day it dawned on me. Writing is writing. No matter what you're writing, it requires lyrical *skill*, as long as words are involved.

26

I consider reading and writing as a way of paying homage to my African ancestors who were never given the chance to partake of such an expression of who they were and what they knew. I can only imagine the rich legacy of the knowledge they might have left behind. So, I am taking up the mantle as one of many of the descendants of slaves, to appreciate and use the opportunity afforded to me through a path that they paved but could not travel. I am encouraging everyone to encourage as many people as you can, to read. If they don't know how, be willing to teach them.

Ignorance is *destroyed by literacy* and *fostered by illiteracy*. A literate people are a strong people. A literate nation is a powerful nation. Also, in order to be a writer with something to say, you must be a reader of those who have said something before you. Nothing in, nothing out.

When traveling through the south, seeing cotton fields, I can sometimes imagine the voices of my ancestors crying out for help and at that time I feel a responsibility to be the very best that I can be. Moments like that and being born and raised in the south, which is the umbilical cord from which African Americans were cut. I feel stronger, and somehow, more connected as an American. It was a heavy price to pay, but the price was paid. I am an American. Not just an African American, but as American as anyone except the Natives of The First Nations.

One thing that plays on my mind is the fact that most of the descendants of the slaves which were brought, forcefully, to this country, *because of their economic status, will never even see the Motherland*. They can't afford to go back home. And what makes me *sad* is, so many, because of the shame and stigma attached to their perception of "The Continent", don't even *want* to visit it. America, if it was your intent to colonize our minds, to a great extent, you have succeeded. *Now is a perfect time for us to break the chains.*

CHAPTER 2

The *Other* Side of Freedom

If you can imagine being freed from slavery into an already hostile atmosphere with no way out, then you can imagine the fear and suffering of the Africans, having just been liberated. Liberated to do what? Wander aimlessly under the elements with no food or a place to lay their heads. Wondering if it's best to stay in groups for safety sake or separate for a better chance at maybe getting some food.

Can you imagine being a man with family members feeling that now you finally have your chance to prove yourself a man, and not even knowing where to start? All the while still confined to the hostile atmosphere of the south, where it all took place and having to beg these same people, who blame *you* for *causing* the war that freed you and tore the land apart.

It makes you wonder how these ex-slaves survived at all. At the same time, I can't help but believe that amongst all of this hostility, was found some understanding and sympathetic hearts among the White people of the south. If not, there was no way they would have survived. Not in the numbers that they did.

Of course, there remained many Whites who took advantage of the former captives in every way possible. Tragedy brings out the best in some, the beast in others. After all, these had recently been *slave* territories.

For the Black race, in America, *true* freedom has *never been realized*. For us, "freedom" comes with so many restrictions that it's hard to even call it *freedom*. You can't live here, you can't work there, why are you driving such an expensive car, how much money are you carrying? These are issues that Black people are having to deal with, on a regular basis. Only someone who feels the hurt can understand the pain. And even then, it's hard to satisfactorily explain to others without having it sound exaggerated.

So, if you ask a Black person, in America, what freedom is like, they can't honestly say. Because we have never truly *been* free in this country. All we can correctly say is that we are freer than we used to be, but the perimeters of our freedom are always shifting over periods of time. Today we can vote, then tomorrow there are new requirements for voting, mostly trying to limit, or prevent African Americans from voting.

Second-class citizenship for Black people is still a reality. In America, as well as in many countries elsewhere in the world. Because it is such a disruptive force, bigotry, more than any other factor, is what is making America unable to move forward, in many ways. Until we can deal with our "Problem" in more honest and realistic ways, we're *never* going to move forward.

"If you just keep sweeping dirt under the carpet; eventually the carpet gets lumpy and the dirt spills out for everyone to see." America's dirt has been exposed to the world and is out in the open for everyone to see. Yet the denials are still being made as the "ruling class" seeks to make it the fault of the oppressed. "Surely, they must have done *something* wrong." When very often, the truth is, they did *nothing* wrong. Except to be in a place where, there are unwritten laws that say African Americans are not supposed to be. Which seems to be *anywhere* in America these days.

In some places this "no Blacks allowed policy" is meant to apply after dark. There are also places where this applies at *all* times. This is where the unwritten responsibilities of police officers seem to be, "Whatever you do. Keep those Blacks in their own areas. We can't afford to have them spilling out into ours. Never know *what* they might do."

And in recent years, it's not just about Blacks, but now includes bigotry toward Muslims and Hispanics, as well. Anyone who is seen as a threat to a White majority in America is being targeted by the system for immigration violations and anything else that could exclude them from becoming citizens of America. Even trying to *take away* their citizenship, by way of loopholes.

Because of the lies that have been told about who contributed what, to the building up of America, coupled with the lack of reading among the citizens, a large number of people believe that the "superior" thinking of White people is what made America the great country that it is. But when you begin to dig deeper, you find that it has been a joint effort from many "superior" minds and from many different races of people who have built America into what it has become. And now that the work is done you can't just send everybody home. For the majority of us, this *is* home. *Bought and paid for*.

And the truth is, America would no longer be as powerful or interesting without us. All of the diversity is what has made and continues to make America great. Not great again, because America has *never stopped* being great. You sold the "American Dream" to all of us and now we want nothing but to enjoy the best that you have to offer.

Citizenship brings with it, the right to vote. In a democratic society voting constitutes power. The answer to circumventing the voting power is to constantly change the process of voting by changing boundaries and anything else that can be done to disqualify voters which could threaten the rich White power structure. Many people, mistakenly, believe that the only reason Dr. Martin Luther King Jr. was assassinated is because he advocated for the rights of Black people. That's true, but only part of the story.

Dr. King was assassinated, ultimately, because he was pointing out the fact that the system at work in America, is against *all* poor people, not just Blacks but poor Whites, as well. When you start to articulate that, and make people realize it, you begin to win them over and anger the ones who don't want them to know. Which is what was happening with Dr. King. Therein lies the danger.

In uniting people of all races, the attention gets shifted toward who the *real* problem is. That would be the oppressive system in full swing in America. *A truly united people become an enemy to the state*. Propaganda will no longer keep them divided. They will ask more pertinent questions like where their tax money is being spent, want to know *why* our enemies *are* our enemies in the first place, and why we should risk dying in some useless war.

A powerful system needs *agents* to help them enforce their agenda, which, in America, comes in the form of the police and, occasionally, the CIA, the FBI, and the military (National Guard at Kent State). All the system needs to do to win them over is drive home the point that without keeping people in line, they become unable to be governed. Some police, being just people like everybody else, start out trying to do the right thing and be fair, in some cases. After encountering the truly criminal element of society, they begin to think, "Wow! If it wasn't for us, these types of people would take over our streets and we can't let that happen." Before long they have ceased to differentiate between *what it looks like* and *what it is*.

In other words, "The last time I dealt with something like this, I had to deal with it in *this* way. So, the same treatment must be applied here." Resulting in sometimes unnecessarily fatal endings when it didn't require the same heavy-handedness because the situations were different *but assumed to be the same.*

Then because of this over-reaction, the police are set upon by an angry public who are looking at all police the same way because they believe them all *to be* the same ruthless, trigger- happy killers. *And some are.*

But just as there are different levels of everyday people, there are different levels of police officers. And the same way people band together in protests against police brutality, police themselves band together for their own safety against perceived danger from a hostile public. Just as criminals are sometimes hiding out among innocent people, crooked cops are sometimes hiding out among descent police officers. A friend, whose opinion I respect, recently said to me, "If a policeman sees another policeman treating someone badly and looks away, pretending he didn't see it. Then he's just as guilty."

One of the more obvious cases of police brutality and miscarriage of justice, was when a Black man, Rodney King, was beaten by members of the Los Angeles Police Department. While a person nearby filmed the whole interaction, which clearly showed police brutality, the jury found them not guilty of any of the charges against them. While the whole world was looking on. America answers to no one, but herself. And most often, she's dishonest.

After slavery was, reluctantly and grudgingly, abolished, (*by law anyway*) came a need for finding ways to keep the former slaves " in their places" while trying help them to assimilate into society. Somewhat.

The answers came in many forms. In the south and even in other parts of the country as well, their "answer" was the Ku Klux Klan. The Klan, as they were affectionately referred to by sympathizers to their cause, used intimidation tactics. Like burning crosses on the property of Black people. This would be an indication that they had been offended, in some way, by a member, or members of that household. It could be for something like moving into the "wrong" (meaning White) neighborhood.

The blame would usually be directed at the male of that particular family and if they didn't heed the warning, it often resulted in injury or death by lynching. *Many* lynchings took place across the south, and elsewhere, throughout America, albeit, more frequently in the south. The hostility toward Black people was fed by the insecurities of Whites and such notions as, "They want to take our jobs."

There were such charges as "reckless eyeballing", meaning a Black man looking at a White woman in a desirous manner. "Undressing her with his eyes," which is self-explanatory. Or is it?

During the height of the lynching period in America, from the emancipation to the late 1940's and even into the early 1950's, there were thousands of Black people, mostly male, but sometimes female also, who were not only lynched in the backwoods by the Ku Klux Klan but in public lynchings as well. As a matter of fact, there were more *public* lynchings, than *private* ones. This was meant to put fear in the Black race. To know that you could be taken from jail, or just grabbed off the street, hung up by a rope around your neck, and often burned alive.

There were many cases where the local authorities would claim they couldn't hold back the "lynch mob" from storming the jails and taking the prisoners out and lynching them publicly. The truth of the matter was, the so-called authorities were, often, willing participants.

In some parts of the country, *and not always the south*, lynching became a sort of pastime where, people would gather at the anticipation of a lynching, bring picnic lunches, and cheer, as the poor soul burned at the end of a rope and eventually fell into the flames. All of this would take place in a celebratory atmosphere, often with their children in tow. Ironically, the purpose was to teach their children that Black people were just animals and not to be thought of as human or civilized, *like White people.*

Many still hold to that belief, even today. To their credit, there were White people who detested slavery and fought against it in whatever way they could. John Brown, a White man who was celebrated in a song which had nothing to do with whom he really was, lead one of the bloodiest slave rebellions in American history. Which included his sons. They were ambushed, and captured, at a place called Harper's Ferry, West Virginia.

The song, "John Brown Had a Little Indian", might have come about to try to diminish his importance and trivialize the fact that a White American put his life on the line, along with his sons, to help free Black people from slavery. The following is a quote by John Brown from a speech that he made during the founding of his militant group The League of Gileadites.

The source for this article: *"John Brown: In His Own Words – Prelude"*. Zikibay.com. Retrieved October 16, 2012.

Before Brown left Springfield in 1850, the United States passed the **Fugitive Slave Act**, a law mandating that authorities in free states aid in the return of escaped slaves and imposing penalties on those who aided in their escape. In response Brown founded a militant group to prevent slaves' capture, the League of Gileadites. In the Bible, **Mount Gilead** was the place where only the bravest of **Israelites** gathered to face an invading enemy.

Brown founded the League with the words, "Nothing so charms the American people as personal bravery. [Blacks] would have ten times the number [of white friends than] they now have were they but half as much in earnest to secure their dearest rights as they are to ape the follies and extravagances of their white neighbors, and to indulge in idle show, in ease, and in luxury. **End of Article**

To paraphrase The Speech: "Nothing gets the attention of Americans as much as personal bravery (standing up for *yourself*). Black people would have ten times the number of White supporters than they have right now if they were but half as serious about pursuing their rights as they are about imitating the foolishness and high living of Whites, and meaningless displays (showing off), being complacent, and trying to live a lavish lifestyle."

"If you get serious about helping yourself, others will be more likely to aid your cause. But when *you* don't show enough willingness to try to change your *own* plight, how can you expect others to?"

White people in other parts of the country, especially those in the north liked to think of themselves as better than southerners, because slavery was confined to the south, but truth be told, most of *them* were also not comfortable around Black people either. That's one of the reasons that incarceration comes so easily to Black people in this country. Locking them up means not having to deal with them.

For a Black *man* living in America, the fear of incarceration looms large, and it has been that way since his arrival in America. The White establishment, which might sound unreal, *even to some White people,* really does exist. And they have laws on the books which were put there to specifically keep Black men "in their place." There is the tactic of treating Black women with disrespect in front of Black men. Making sexual innuendos toward them in the presence of their man. That is meant to provoke him into doing something that could get him arrested or charged with a crime, knowing that if he does nothing, he looks weak in the eyes of his woman.

In a woman's mind, her man is supposed to protect her from other men. And in a man's mind his woman is supposed to belong, sexually, to only him. There have been many other ways in which each have felt that they were left disrespected by someone and not been properly protected by their spouses.

There are ways that White men speak to Black men in front of Black women which is meant to demean the Black man. And the Black man, because of the threat of losing their job, going to jail, or worse, often are unable to properly respond, which naturally, brings a feeling of loss of respect from his woman. This tactic tends not to work as well with the newer generations of Black men who are less afraid of incarceration and generally don't care about the "White man's rules."

There are people, Black and White, who say that young Black men don't want to work for a living. This, naturally, is true with *some* young people of *all* races. Older ones too. On the other hand, *one* of the reasons for a shortage of jobs for Black men is that sometimes White men, in charge of hiring, don't want Black men working in the same place as White men because of the potential for confrontation. The relationship between Black men and White men is one that, unless they are friends, or are on a friendly basis, can be a very precarious one.

Although living in separate communities, it was inevitable that the two races came in contact with each other. The local general store where *everyone* shopped, was called general because it carried everything that the community needed. All in one place. This made it a type of meeting place, where people could socialize and exchange information.

Women were allowed to converse with women of the opposite race, to a certain extent. These conversations produced ideas about women's issues such as trading cooking styles, sewing, and fashion ideas.

Conversations between *White men* and *Black men* were kept to a minimum. Distrust of the White man was understandable on the part of the Black man, because of the dangers that they faced for even the most minor infraction. Such as Blacks looking into the eyes of Whites and failing to look at the ground when in the presence of a White person. There were laws that became known as "Jim Crow", written to specifically keep the Black and White citizens apart. Laws that, within themselves, treated the Black race as second - class citizens.

The main reason that the southern Whites didn't trust *Blacks* was because of guilt and fear of reprisal for enslaving them and bringing them to America. And *some* of their hatred was because they weren't quite ready to *give up* slavery, since it provided the slave owners with free labor and free sex. Which consisted of the rape of slave women whenever they felt the urge, and on some occasions, the raping of men and children also.

There was a perception, by Black people, that if they could live "up North", they would somehow fare better. This was true to a certain extent, because slavery had been confined to the southern states. This meant that it would be more difficult to be accepted as anything but a slave, by former slave owners, who never really wanted them freed in the *first* place.

Whatever wages were earned by Blacks in the south, were meagre, at best. One of the reasons was that, with the abolishment of slavery, the south's industry, mostly cotton, collapsed. With the Black people having no work and nowhere to go, some Whites offered a new type of existence to them. Very much akin to slavery in some ways, it was labeled as "sharecropping."

A sharecropper is a person living on the property of, and in a house (usually, a shack) owned by another person. Raising crops and " sharing" the proceeds with the owners of the property. The "sharing" was, in most cases, one-sided in favor of the property owner, keeping the sharecropper in debt. This usually kept increasing from year to year, leaving the tenant in escalating debt to the property owner. Remember that most Black people, since fresh out of slavery, couldn't read, write or count so they didn't know if they were being cheated or not.

The property owner would often remind the sharecropper about just how "lenient" he, the owner, had been with the sharecropper by not demanding the entire debt be paid all at once. Of course, there was always "next year" to look forward to catching up. Since the sharecropper was in debt to the property owner, it gave the owner the right to keep the sharecropper there until his debt was paid off. Or risk going to prison.

The owners would sometimes use intimidation tactics, involving the local police to reinforce the threat. Because sharecroppers had their families with them, there was no chance of skipping out, owing the property owner, and risking the loss of their family. In some cases, the *entire* family would be part of the contract with the landowner, leaving *all* of them with no way out of the obligation until the debt was paid off. Which sometimes was never. Are you sensing a new form of slavery?

It was not just Black people who were kept in bondage through sharecropping though. Poor Whites sometimes found themselves in the very same predicament. Being White, however, to their way of thinking, still placed them above their Black counterparts. In fact, they, poor Whites, were a large part of the Ku Klux Klan's membership. Not really seeing *themselves* as victims. Although, in many ways, they were.

Those Black southerners who were fortunate enough to make it, "up the road", as up north was sometimes referred to, found that in some ways, things were only slightly better than "down south". However, those who could do so left the south in droves. Settling in places like Chicago, Detroit, Baltimore, Washington, D.C., New York and Philadelphia.

After a while the so-called liberal minded Whites of the north, began to feel the strain of having these uneducated aliens in their midst. The general consensus was "You can live in the city, but these are your boundaries." And even in cities like New York and Chicago these rules were enforced. Sometimes to the point of death. Even today in some of the northern cities, there are "no Blacks allowed" areas. Many will deny it, and it's not posted, but we *know* it's true.

Black people had to learn to hustle in order to make a life for themselves. Some men shined shoes, worked as elevator operators, in factories, as train porters, wherever they could find work. Others turned to illegal means of support, like gambling, pimping, and dealing drugs.

Women turned to some of the types of work that they had become accustomed to, from slavery. Cooking, cleaning, taking in laundry, and babysitting. They would work during the day, but by nightfall they would have to be out of those areas and back to their own.

In some respects, not much had changed. Boundaries, called "red lining", were well understood. Straying past that imaginary "red line" could bring harm to Black people. Even *after* slavery, night traveling in the south was done, by Blacks, only in cases of emergencies, because Whites, known as "nightriders", patrolled the roads looking for Black people to "make an example of". These "examples" came in the form of beatings, rapes, torturing, and lynching.

The so-called Negros of the north were a type of experiment, to see how well they could, or would, assimilate into life after slavery. Things began to work out alright, as long as they " recognized their place." The job of keeping them in their place was given to, and became the priority of local law enforcement.

As a rule, police in America have always had a rocky relationship with citizens of the Black community. And still do. But contrary to rumor, I have found no concrete, historic evidence to support the belief that policing in America was begun for the purpose of catching runaway slaves.

Whites lived far enough apart from Blacks, yet close enough to keep an eye on whatever they were doing. In order to maintain the upper hand, some Whites felt it necessary to intimidate Blacks by burning crosses on their property, and sometimes even *confiscating* the property of Blacks who were fortunate enough to obtain a piece of land.

In order to make their position of intimidation more official, White men formed the Ku Klux Klan to instill fear in the recently freed former slaves. The Ku Klux Klan still exists today, but without nearly as much power and freedom to intimidate African Americans, publicly. Racism today usually comes in more subtle ways, which can be denied as *even being* racism.

I can't help but believe that even the breakdown in many relationships between the Black man and Black woman are still rooted in slavery and the bigotry that they have experienced *since* slavery. Can a man(slave) overcome the fact that another man(slaveowner) can walk in and take away his wife/woman and have sex with her anytime he pleases. On the other hand, how can a woman *respect* a man who *allows* this to happen. One would have to look at the facts and search deep within themselves to not hold resentment.

After keeping Black people enslaved in America for well over three hundred years, their White oppressors looked for ways, during slavery, *and* after emancipation, to keep them *mentally* enslaved. One of their main objectives was to try to make Black people hate themselves *and* each other. Another practice which was used during, *and* after slavery, by Whites, was to openly, prefer the light- skinned "Negro" to the dark-skinned "Negro." Fostering a sense of entitlement in the lighter complexioned Black people and prompting a feeling of hatred toward them, from the darker complexioned ones.

The intent was to make them feel, the lighter the skin color, the closer you were to being White. Of course, neither group was accepted as anything but a Negro by Whites. Still it kept them bickering and preoccupied among themselves. Which was the whole idea. *Internal* bigotry, so to speak.

There are arguments, about race, between Black people that are still causing friction among us to this day. For example (and this is something that Black people themselves more than likely came up with, because of their resentment of the "White establishment") a Black person who speaks the English language fluently is sometimes referred to as "talking White."

A much more serious problem is, when Black students apply themselves to paying attention and having the correct answers in class, they're often labeled as "*acting* White" by other Black students, as if being intelligent is not a Black trait.

In order to dominate a race of people, if you can make them believe that you're smarter than they are and that your ways of doing things are better than theirs, you have a greater chance of succeeding. As you look around the world, to places where the indigenous people have been displaced and colonized, you will see that some of them tend to have a certain amount of admiration for their colonizers. Seeing *them* as winners and *themselves* as losers. In America, the admiration is *obviously* mutual between the races. Maybe it is not declared *openly*, but the *evidence* is there in so many ways.

Having pride is much more realistic when you have something to base it on. Take away a person's identity and you have a better chance of controlling them. It's much easier to keep someone down if they are unaware of any achievements made by people with whom they identify as being their own.

The slaves were constantly being told that they were subhuman until *some* of them, accepted this to be true. Often helping to perpetuate the stereotype, by trying to distance themselves from anything identifying with Africa. Many began to aspire to anything of European origin, and to shun, with disdain, anything African.

Some African Americans, even to this day, accuse others of being too "Black" and not *"cultured"* enough, if they don't accept the "White" way of doing things. Nothing gets the job of assimilation done as well as the people who have accepted the oppressor's lifestyle, because they help to promote it in a more *direct* way. It becomes harder to reject something when it appears that everybody else is doing it. You begin to stand out and become a target. Trying to avoid this, the holdouts often give in and start to do as everyone else is doing.

When people are living among each other and having a chance to see and hear the things that capture their imaginations, it's going to be reflected in their lifestyles. Crossing culture lines is inevitable in *any* social situation.

That same habit of races "borrowing" from each other continues to this day. In America and everywhere else around the world. It seems to be a human trait. The one who has the power, makes the rules. In this "New World" the Europeans had all of the power because they brought the Africans over as slaves, and they either already had, or were in the process of (depending on the time in history) committing genocide against the Native people or bringing them under submission. So, to the oppressor, being emulated by the oppressed people, must have made them feel that the brainwashing process was working well.

There were, and still are, many ways in which this brainwashing affected Black people. One sign was when Black people started referring *to themselves* using the n-word. Some Black people still use that word to describe each other until this day, with many excuses, though none satisfactorily, to justify its use. "By using it ourselves, it takes the sting out of it." "It has become a term of endearment." "We can say it, but *they* can't." Some have even begun to refer to their friends, fondly, as "my n-word." I wonder if they've even considered the fact that the slaveholders used that very same phrase when referring to the slaves? "My n-words".

During slavery, a practice among neighboring plantations was to stage a fight between the two strongest Black men from each plantation. It would be a fight to the death, with no weapons involved. There could be only one survivor, or they would both be killed. They had to kill or be killed. The "winner" would most often kill their opponent by biting him in the jugular vein, which would make him bleed to death.

The saddest thing about this is, the practice of Black men killing each other has remained with us and risen to a phenomenal level. Black men, especially younger Black men and teenagers have become the most prolific, for lack of a better word, killing machine in America. It has roots in slavery.

Reasons are being offered, like, "frustration causes people to strike out at the ones closest to them." "The Black community is being flooded with drugs and guns, from outside sources." "The very high volume of robberies is because of the *economic* situation in Black communities." Black People have always been, and remain, in a catch 22 situation in this country. And even though, all of the above is true, our attitudes toward this type of thinking have to change if we are going to survive.

Even though slavery has been such a profound part of Black peoples' history in America, bringing much misery, it still cannot be blamed for *all* of the present-day ills of the Black race in America. And although racism still plays a major role in the misery of present-day Blacks, there is yet, a real need for self-examination in our relationships to each other. For instance, a situation has emerged in the Black community where the grownups have lost control and become afraid of the younger generations. Sometimes even *our own children*.

With too many in law enforcement adopting the attitude of, "If *you* can't raise them, *don't expect us to*. So, call us when things get out of hand." Very often, by this time, the force that they come with, is deadly. Few people, of *any* race, are willing to speak frankly on these issues (out of control youth *and* police brutality). But until we do, things are only going to get worse. Speak to anyone who is willing to weigh in on this situation and most of them will offer a simple solution. "They just need to get off their butts and go to work." "Lock them all up." Which seems to be the general consensus, but there are no simple solutions.

We, as a country, are badly in need of meaningful dialogue between many different cross sections of our American society. Law enforcement, citizens, government, educators, races. Everyone has a stake in this. One big problem though is that we're so long overdue that we are all to the point of being *fed up* with each other. With many of our thoughts about points of debate, being biased and steadfast, because of seeing and putting up with so much, for so long, that it's hard to keep an open mind. And that includes *all* of us.

It has become plain to see that the lessons of self- hatred taught to Blacks from slavery have been so well received that they have extended *beyond* the era of slavery. But that is not to be naïve about the hatred still being directed toward us from *outside* of our community. There are some people of the White community who want to blame Black Americans, Mexican Americans, and Muslim Americans for all of *their* problems, as well.

So busy pointing out the faults of the non-White races that they overlook the *contributions* being made by them. Like the jobs performed by the Mexican Americans that are so important to the agriculture of America and to the construction industry, as well.

The argument is that these jobs have been *taken over* by Mexican immigrants, when the reality is that so many of these jobs have been *passed over* by other Americans who felt that they were too good to do such *menial* labor. There was a time, in the not so distant past, when Italian Americans were discriminated against, for the same reasons that Mexican Americans *presently* are.

Because so many things are vying for the attention of American citizens, not getting enough rest is a major factor in the decrease of output from the workplace sector of America, a fact which is *majorly overlooked*. If a person is not able to relax and take time to think, then they are not really at their best, having less energy *and* brainpower to offer.

America has become a sleep-deprived nation because of a lifestyle which requires most people to have to work harder to keep up with the pace of survival and do it on a minimal amount of sleep. That work, and stress load is intensified if you're a person of color, especially Black. Because you have the burden of racism to shoulder, as well.

During the years after WWII, there was an attitude of thriving and winning in America. Because the Black man had shown his commitment to his country by going to war and doing his fair share to help win it, some things were open to us. As always, *on a limited basis*. Never-the-less, we were able to get a better education, and sometimes better jobs, than *before* the war.

Not everyone was pleased with this. And when the schools were required to begin integration, White America's true colors came out. With Black children having to have armed military personnel escorting them to school. As if that wasn't enough, the colleges and schools of higher learning went even further to try to keep out Black students.

Having already discovered that education is the key to a better life, Black students, and parents, were willing to go through whatever it took to achieve that goal. To the point of putting their lives on the line. And some lives were lost in the process. These were times which ushered in strong Black leaders like Martin Luther King Jr., Malcolm X, Stokely Carmichael, H. Rap Brown, Angela Davis, Fannie Lou Hamer, and others.

These were strong men and women who were willing to do whatever it took to allow Black people to gain access to a decent education, better jobs, and a decent place to live and raise a family.

Thankfully, there were a number of Whites who felt the same way. Realizing that a good citizen is better than a bad one. In other words, education and a decent job can create a person who is more able to contribute to society and ultimately to the country. Some politicians, Black *and* White realized that without Black people receiving certain basic rights, this country was headed for strife and even more bloodshed than they had seen before.

In 1963 President John F. Kennedy, recognizing the need to calm down the Black population following the riots of the spring of 1963, proposed the Civil Rights Act, on behalf of the disenfranchised people in America, to outlaw discrimination based on race, color, religion, sex, or national origin. Granting equal access to public places and employment, enforcing desegregation of schools and the right to vote.

Not surprisingly, the bill was opposed by a filibuster in the Senate. After President Kennedy's assassination on November 22 in the fall of that same year, Lyndon B. Johnson, his successor, put the bill before the Congress and The Senate as a perfect way to honor the memory of our assassinated President.

The Senate voted 73-27 in favor of it. The House of Congress voted 289-126 in favor of it. So, on July 2, 1964 the Civil Rights Act of 1964 was signed into law by President Lyndon B. Johnson in the White House. If you will notice the numbers for and against the bill, you will see that not everyone supported the disenfranchised peoples' "Constitution" of sorts. Some things never change but although we keep that in mind, we can't let those type of truths rule our thinking. In fact, just the opposite.

We must rise above that type of thinking. In our own minds and especially when it comes from others. I refuse to donate any of my time to thinking about someone who wishes for me to fail. Stumbling blocks are made to go over, *or around them*. Many have come before me and given their lives for me to be where I am. I honor them by achieving as many positive goals as I can, by dedication and honest hard work.

I have resigned myself to the fact that there will always be obstacles in my path and people who hate for me to succeed, but my love for success overrules their hatred of me. To be very honest, when I first learned of Dr. Martin Luther King Jr. around 1961 or 62, his thinking did not appeal to me.

Someone who would let people beat him down, sic dogs on him, spit on him, and use the full force of water hoses on him wasn't the type of person that I aspired to be. I still don't. I'm not a Dr. King. But I found out that he was right for the time and couldn't have achieved it any other way. In my mind he is nothing less than a great man.

Almost as soon as the Civil Rights Act was passed drugs began to creep into the Black community. And not long after that they were *flooding* the Black community with drugs. Who *they* are is an argument that is yet raging but it's obvious that *someone* seems to think that a Black mind is *not* such a terrible thing to waste. We must get past the point of proving them right, by taking the bait. The world is waiting to shake hands with strong Black men like President Barak Obama.

If the city governments are going to allow a liquor store on every corner of every street in Black neighborhoods, then it's *my* responsibility to teach my children not to patronize that store. Of course, that means I must lead by example. It stands to reason that *an irresponsible person will have trouble teaching another person how to behave responsibly.*

The use of drugs and alcohol have been one of the leading causes of death in the Black community for decades. This is no accident. They are strategically placed there for the purpose of keeping Black people dependent. Dependent on the drugs, alcohol, the welfare system. Look at it this way. If you're medicated from drugs or alcohol, it's impossible to hold down a job. Still those who readily supply you with these things will point to you and say, "See there I told you they were no good, shifty, and lazy."

In today's society, there are thousands of ways to get inside someone's head. Through media, television, suggestive conversation, music, books, and many other ways. Even when you're not being programmed you could still be participating in something that is just not productive for you to be doing. Maybe watching other peoples' lives on reality shows. Where is that taking *you*? Do you even *want* to achieve anything or just *watch others succeed?*

How much is playing video games going to do for *your* future? Think of the person who is designing the game. They've got you waiting to see what kind of game they will come up with next to occupy your *unprecious time.* When you are not using your time constructively your detractors are winning because as long as you're distracted, you're not living up to your potential and they always know that you won't get very far.

You might say, "What is in a name? Is a name really that important?" A name is what we identify with and *how* we are identified by others. African people since being brought to America by way of slavery have transitioned through more name changes than probably anyone on planet earth.

From the beginning we were referred to as Africans, then Negros, Blacks, darkies, the n-word, colored, Afro American, and finally African American. Depending on who is describing us, all of these names are still being used to refer to our people. Of course, some are used in privacy.

What others call you is not as important as what you call yourself. If someone calls you a dirty name and you don't accept it, the affect that it has on you is limited because of your rejection of it. On the other hand, if you start calling yourself by that name, they have defeated you in at least two ways. First, they have the satisfaction of knowing that you have given up, in spirit, and accepted it. Secondly, they know that now you think of yourself in the way that they have described you. *Whether consciously or unconsciously.*

This is where that "word" comes in for serious discussion and examination. To my recollection, there is no word on earth that is used to name a people that is as derogatory as the n-word. Knowing this, I refuse to perpetuate it by using it. This, the most disgusting way on earth to describe someone has been made "acceptable" by the same people whom it was created to denigrate. Black people. It was created by White bigots and given new life and longevity by the people it was intended to hurt. Black people.

Some older Black people blame the "come back" of the word on the younger generation, especially "those rappers". They say that the young people are to blame for its newfound acceptance. Even to the point that White people, especially young rap fans, are using the word "affectionately". Let's be clear. The origin of the word was meant to hurt and demean. It still does that in the minds of conscious people of any race, especially the Black race.

Getting back to how the rappers were able to latch on to the word so handily, is to admit that it was never really missing from the Black community at any time, *anyway*. Even as James Brown was urging us to, "Say it loud. I'm Black and I'm proud!", we were still referring to each other as n-words. *Maybe* even Mr. Brown himself was using the word.

One fact about my people, we are generally loud. It's an African trait as far as I can tell. So, *whatever* we say, it's usually loud. Just for the record that is not necessarily negative. But anyone observing Black Americans over the years can attest to the fact that the n-word has been used in so many ways by Black people themselves that it sounds almost hypocritical to complain about other races using that word to describe us.

Curtis Mayfield, one of the greatest songwriters of our time, wrote songs like, "We're A Winner" and "Keep On Pushing", strong Black anthems, meant to sustain us during the civil rights struggles. Yet, later in his career, while composing the soundtrack for the movie, "Superfly", he used the n-word numerous times. This is not meant to imply that he was contradicting himself. He was just wise enough to know that if you want to reach the people with what you're doing, you need to relate to how they are living. In this case, the language that they use.

It is unfortunate that such a word has become so much a part of the fabric of who the Black community is. Some even hold that word so dear that they get angry when anyone says that we should stop using it. "Ain't nothing wrong with that! It's a part of who we are." Sadly, *too much* a part of who we are. It is going to be a long and tedious journey trying to rid ourselves of the affinity that many of us have with that word, but it's time for the journey to begin.

One thing is for sure in America, if enough people use a word for so long, it becomes legitimate and will soon wind up in the dictionaries. The British hate that about us, "re-inventing the Queen's English." One such word is, "ain't". I well remember when the use of that word would draw a frown from many people within earshot. It is now legitimately used for phrases such as: "are not", "am not", "is not", and possibly more. Oh, and it's in the dictionary too.

Another word that was disdained is, "y'all". Meaning, "you all" or, "all of you." Being from the southern part of the country I remember spending time with part of my family living in Philadelphia. One thing that stands out most was how people there would laugh and say, "You must be from the south," when I would say, "y'all".

Now they're saying it all over the country. There is another thing that I'm happy to see. And that is how African Americans from the northern states have gotten over the feeling of being "better" than southern African Americans. They've even begun to show appreciation for their southern heritage.

64
You Might *Think* You Want This!

Sometimes being Black in America feels like a crime within itself. To be singled out for no apparent reason. Other than, someone committed a crime who "looks a lot like you." Black people in America can give countless examples of being, not only detained, but harassed, by the police. Only to be told, "Sorry to inconvenience you, but we're just doing our job." Sadly enough, that's all too true.

In so many cities, towns, and communities in America, the *job* of the police is to *control the presence of Black people.* Making sure their presence is minimal, if at all, in these areas. In the meantime, other races are getting away with crimes by not being on their radar. And even when they're caught, they're still treated better.

Since the styles and, quite a few habits of Black Americans are "copied and pasted" throughout the world by non-Blacks and even Blacks from other countries, it is no surprise that some people express a "desire" to be Black, even when they are not. That is, they desire the "*hipness*" of being Black but have no desire to bear the "*burden.*" There are even Black Americans who try to conveniently "act *White*" when the opportunity presents itself, trying to escape the "heavy" side of being Black.

There are also those who express the "I wish I were Black" sentiment while trying to show solidarity with our plight, knowing that the burden that is put on Black people will never be theirs, because of their birthright. The truth is, "You don't *want* this weight that most of *us* struggle beneath."

Many burdens carried by people in Black communities, are non-existent and not even given a second thought in other communities. Things like having such a disproportionate number of liquor stores in the Black and poor neighborhoods which greatly contributes to the alcoholism of those communities. Being so conveniently located creates a direct temptation to someone who has a weakness for alcohol and are waging a battle against it.

As for the curious, they are *always* there to entice *them*, "just in case you're wondering." Studies have shown that a large percentage of the time, alcohol addiction leads to drug addiction. So, the question which begs to be answered is: "Who, but someone who doesn't have Black peoples' best interest at heart, would think it's okay to flood them with liquor stores?"

How could we ever forget what happened to the Native people of this land, after being plied with alcohol? With Black people the ante has been upped. It's no longer just alcohol, but drugs, as well. And they are doing *real* damage. Contributing to the murder rates, suicide rates, robberies, rapes, and most of the other negative things going on inside of the world of most Black Americans. And sadly, some of us have chosen to make that culture look alluring by feeding into the stereotype.

This is how the situation has gone. You have set a trap for me and my people, through drugs, alcohol, movies, music, etc. Some of my people have taken the bait and made it look enticing. Your young people have seen this and decided that they want in on it, because it's "cool". But now you're upset with *me* for turning them out. If you had not perpetrated this, in the first place, everyone would have been better off, and our country could be about the business of making *everyone* a good citizen.

Once again though, not much, *good or bad*, affects one community without affecting the other. It's only a matter of time before things spill over, out of one community into the other. On the brighter side, Black people, on a whole, have learned to survive in this hostile climate of American living.

In many ways, they have taken the lemons that they were given and turned them to lemonade. And after the lemonade has been made, it has been sampled by those from outside of the Black community, wondering, "How did you achieve that, with almost nothing? But I like it. Can I borrow it? I'll make a few changes and when you get it back, you might not recognize it. And it will certainly have *my name on it*."

Another of the burdens of being Black in America is sometimes the inability to gain employment even while being the most *employable*. And when finally getting employed, being kept at the lowest end of the pay scale. The threat of incarceration is also a constant threat for the Black male. Sometimes for crimes not even committed by them. Though I'm not saying that there are no criminal elements in the Black communities of America. There are plenty. And I don't believe that I'm exaggerating by saying that a *lot* of things connected to the criminal element in the Black community have to do with economics.

The thinking is, "I have to make money somehow." I'm not defending criminal behavior, but just citing some possible reasons for it. Whether it's drug dealing, prostitution, or robbery, to name a few.

The people committing these crimes are often doing so as a means of supporting themselves. Well why can't they just get jobs?! Many of them have criminal records which won't permit them to be meaningfully employed. *So, who made them commit the crimes in the first place? Nobody forced them!*

The harsh reality is that sometimes a simple mistake or lapse of good judgement can adversely affect you for the rest of your life. And because being Black is often thought of as synonymous with being criminal, the court system sees Black people as habitual "screw-ups." As a result, sentencing is very often harsher than that of criminals of other races who have committed the same, or similar crimes. There is a certain amount of bigotry involved in handing down sentencing in the judiciary system in America.

Stiff sentences handed down to African American offenders intended to rid the streets of these "criminal elements," are *often* unfair. And because these "criminal elements" are grandfathers, fathers, brothers, uncles, and sons, a dent is left in the communities in the way of mentoring and teaching the young ones coming after. Meaning the community and eventually, the country, suffers as a result of these unfair practices.

Of course, if you were to ask someone who is a member of the judiciary, they will tell you that they're "fair at all Times." "These people deserved every bit of time that they got." "I run an unbiased courtroom." But history *testifies against them.*

CHAPTER 3

Inferiority Is Complex

America has the potential to be anything it chooses to be. It's sad that it chooses to be divided according to race, religion, and various other aspects, with race causing the biggest division. It's strange how we can come together for sporting events, share the same love for television programs, movies, rub shoulders in the workplace but then exist as separate, polarized races. Except for those who break ranks with the status quo and say, "I'm going to give you the benefit of the doubt and treat you according to what I see from you and not what I've been told about you."

Which very often gets them ostracized and called a "n-word lover", if they're White and befriending a Black person. Because of the shunning and threat of being labelled, some who would befriend me, decide to leave me alone, rather than be subjected to this. After realizing it, many African Americans get fed up and assume that all White people feel that they are better than Black people and leave them alone altogether. And it appears that this is what *many* White people want.

At times, I've heard Black people exclaim, "I never even knew this place was here," while discovering a "White" neighborhood tucked away somewhere and hidden from plain sight. There are many of these getaways in almost every town and city. Getting away from Black people. Anytime a Black face shows up there, it had better be for a very short time, or else the police or neighborhood patrol starts cruising around. Pretty soon, you're being questioned about what you are doing there. Often coming with a warning to not be caught in that area again.

I've wondered if it's *fear* of me, *or just plain hatred* of me and other Black people. It most often feels like hatred. If it's fear, the irony begs to be noted. *I'm not the one who has hunted down, tortured and killed people because they didn't look like me.*

Some who advocate on the side of "White flight", as it's called, say "Clean up your neighborhoods and maybe we won't *have* to avoid you." When the reality is, many poor people, *White and Black*, who are living in squalor, have a defeated attitude and really couldn't care less about anything but a welfare check which provides food and a place to sleep. And sadly, that's where the system wants them.

The reality is White people who move up in financial status can escape *their* "white trash" status, but the *Black race* is labelled as *all* being "ghetto-minded." And it often doesn't matter how much money or education you have. Sometimes the more education and money you have, the more hated you are. It isn't fair by any means, but it is the bare- naked truth. There are exceptions to every rule, but generally that is the thinking which applies.

The word ghetto, first used to describe the Jewish neighborhoods in Poland, namely Warsaw, during the war and pre-war eras, has become a new, and negative, way of describing anything associated with being Black or inferior. If a car is badly in need of repair, or a paint job, it can be referred to as being "so ghetto." Speaking in a certain dialect often gets the admonition, *"Stop talking so ghetto."* Dressing a certain way can draw comments like, *"That looks so ghetto!"*

Once again, the inference is that black is negative and white is positive. For instance, referring to a lie as, "a little white lie", is meant to make it sound less harmful. The phrase, "All American", in case you haven't noticed, is another way of referring to someone White. And if you are not White, it's meant to make you feel left out.

These are some of the things that are ingrained in the American psyche. So much so, that even Black people themselves can be heard using some of these idioms. "Like the pot calling the kettle black." Any way you slice this statement it means, to be black is negative. I happen to like black, and since I *am Black*, I will never see it as being bad.

Sometimes Black people get that "But you're different" treatment and are given a chance. This can leave the benefactor with the feeling of, "I'm not against *all* Blacks. I just needed to find the right one." I can accept that. Because it sometimes brings about a, "Let me examine before I judge," attitude. Which is a start, and at least gives a person a chance to be seen, as who they are.

While we are *building* walls *around the country*, we *should be tearing down* the walls *between the citizens*. What are we protecting? It's more like preserving. Preserving the *American* way of life. Which, if you're non-White, is not so great. The *most direct* threat to America's well-being exists, *not outside* of her borders, but *within them*. And it doesn't have to be that way.

Even our churches are mostly segregated. Although it's not true for *every* church, on Sunday mornings America's churches are said to be the most segregated institutions in the country. "In God We Trust." But obviously not in His Word, which tells us to love our fellow man and woman. Think about it. Whether you're White or Black, when was the last time that you saw a person of a different race at your place of worship?

Since I don't want this book getting bogged down in religious and political debates, which could steal from the point that I'm *really* trying to make, that is all that I'm going to say about this. America is full of promise and potential. But promise and potential left on the launching pad, and unfulfilled, are sadder than if they were never known about in the first place.

We've been through foreign wars together. And have won most of them. Yet, when it comes to Black and White soldiers it seems that as soon as we set foot on American soil, "You go your way and I'll go mine. And if you see me anywhere, don't act like you know me. My people wouldn't understand."

We make songs about living in harmony (*Ebony and Ivory*), television shows (*Miami Vice, I Spy*), movies (*Lethal Weapon, Guess Who's Coming to Dinner*) but in real life we just can't seem to get it together. We pass laws against discrimination and vow to fight against every bigoted action that anyone could take against a fellow American.

Then it's all pushed aside when we remember who we *really* are. After tragic incidents we have candlelight vigils, hug, join arms, sing, and pray together and agree to *work* together to prevent future tragedies. Then most of us go our separate ways, *until the next tragedy*.

We *claim* to be the most civilized country in the world, but we *display* the opposite, in many ways. We criticize other countries because of the amount of violence that their governments use to suppress their people. But there is no other country in the world with as much *citizen on citizen* violence as there is in America. Across the board.

While the debate is over certain weapons that are being used to commit mass murder, not much is being said about trying to change the mindset of Americans, as a whole. Which is the *real* problem.

But then, we're so busy *being* American that we fail to even *believe* that we *can* change. In some strange way, we *anticipate* the next big tragedy. And wouldn't dare admit to feeling that way because it would make us seem psychotic. And to some degree, we are.

Living in such a complex country makes us that way. Always having to negotiate our way through abnormal situations has made us have to become psycho analysts in order to survive. Living on the edge, hoping for the best, but always leaving room for, and expecting, the worst.

We have Black people killing other Black people, almost as if it's a sport. And Black people being killed by police at an alarming rate, especially considering the fact they're sworn to serve and protect *all of us*. We have a domestic violence problem, in all of the races, where men, most often White (with the numbers of Blacks increasing), kill their whole families. Spouses *and* children.

Mass murders committed in places where large numbers of people gather, have skyrocketed in recent years. Then probably the saddest of all, are the school shootings, where innocent children and young adults are chosen as random targets. With some calling it, "fake news", without even realizing that if it were indeed fake news, the people in that town or city would be the first to say it isn't true. Maybe they are just afraid to face the fact that people can truly be that evil.

On the other hand, there are shows like *The Academy Awards*, *The American Music Awards*, *The Golden Globe Awards*, *The Billboard Awards*, *The Soul Train Awards* and *The Grammy Awards* bringing people together in grand fashion.

Those in attendance at the actual shows sometimes get to rub shoulders with their fellow stars and be seen by those watching by way of television, acting as if everything in their life is wonderful. And sometimes it is.

These presentations go to great lengths to outdo their previous performances, with the intention of impressing everyone in attendance and those watching by television. Larger than life is the American way. But then, like a lot of things in America, these things promise but don't deliver.

We make movies and shows about the perfect life, but we can't, *or won't*, solve that nagging problem of getting along racially, or socially. I guess those few hours of *virtual* harmony and happiness are better than nothing at all. If not, that's too bad because in America that's as good as it gets.

The American promise of providing a better life has drawn immigrants from all parts of the world. Some brilliant and some not so brilliant, but hard workers, who have done their share of building America up. If immigrants allowed into this country are *from European countries,* they are most often allowed to assimilate without problems.

They are given opportunities that Black people, even those with generations of history in America, could only dream of. And then they rub it in by saying things like, "My grandfather came here from the old country with $2.00 in his pocket, worked a fruit stand and now he's wealthy. So, what's holding your people back?"

In many cases the answer would be, a "skin problem", meaning, a problem with others accepting the skin I'm in.

It's not hard imagining a Black man or woman *having* a fruit stand. What's hard is imagining them being *supported,* by clientele. Even some Black people tend to be more supportive of White establishments than Black ones because they have been taught to believe that their own race is inferior.

But a Black person who gets the opportunity to visit a country like Jamaica or Nigeria, where there is a majority Black population, are often in culture shock to see Black people owning thriving businesses of the sort that they might *never* see them own in America.

In this country, if a Black man acquires a job making an honest living, there are many who will do everything in their power to make sure he loses it. One of the most popular methods is through confrontation, which, when we stand our ground, allows them to say, "See I told you. He can't get along with anybody. All they know is violence." When *provocation* was at the *core* of the disturbance.

In order to counter this type of treatment, in the name of fairness, affirmative action has been introduced. And though it *appears to mean well*, it invokes resentment from non-Blacks who feel that Black People *now have an unfair advantage.*

It also serves the purpose of making us look like we need help competing. But its' saving grace is that it has helped some of our people in ways which, without it, they could not have achieved. Truth is, it's trying to make up for opportunities which were denied to us.

The same criticism is leveled at us for Black people having their own month, albeit the shortest one in the year, to celebrate *Black* history. Which begs the question, how can we be on the same planet and have a separate history from everyone else? It's twofold: 1) By giving Black people their own month, it brings about resentment from the other races, 2) By *condensing* the accomplishments of Black people. *Our complete contributions are too numerous to fit into that time slot*, so they're simply left out. Leaving Black people and everyone else to believe that all we amount to is what you see us as today, and of course, slavery.

We must *study* if we're serious about learning the truth. If you are not already a reader, you might be pleasantly surprised to know how much information can be gained from reading certain books. But just like everything else in life. You will need to be selective.

If you know that you *came from* knowledgeable people, it gives you a base of strength from which to build. When you are *unaware of the accomplishments* of your people, it can take away from the motivation that propels you to reach higher. A sure way to shut a people down is to make them feel like they are non-contributors and reinforce that fact, by deleting their history.

You then must start from scratch, which puts you *behind* those who are in touch with, and building on, the developments of *their* ancestry. Allowing you to feel disenfranchised and inferior. To rob a people of their culture, is to rob them of their hope. When robbed of your hope, you must manufacture your own.

Being not so many years removed from slavery, during the early part of the twentieth century until the middle of it, put Black people at many disadvantages. Lack of education, no sense of direction for fear of appearing disrespectful or too high minded, no money to invest in themselves, and the threat of being lynched for the smallest perceived infraction against a White person. Many were murdered for things that they didn't do but were falsely *accused* of doing.

Although Black *women* were also the targets of White racism, it was the Black *man* who received the harshest treatment. Black *women* were often hired to do the domestic work. Cooking, cleaning, and babysitting. This served a purpose in making the Black man feel inadequate by giving his woman work and leaving him unemployed. To make matters worse, the wives were reminded, often, about "That no good lazy man of yours."

Some Black women adopted this same attitude toward their men, not realizing that it was meant to drive a wedge between the man and woman, destabilizing the family structure. Part of the reason that Black men couldn't get work was because too many White men didn't want them being in stable positions, having the ability to care for their families. Thereby leaving the family *unstable*. An attitude which is sometimes still prevalent in today's workplace.

Suppressing Black peoples' accomplishments and contributions are only *a part* of the plan of oppression, a more direct assault is doing things like flooding the Black communities with drugs and alcohol, which they have become accustomed to readily consuming in large quantities. So, whose fault is it, really? Ultimately their own. We *have* the option to walk away or refuse to participate.

How many years, can you fall for the same old trick, and blame it on someone else? If every time you stick your hand into the fire, it burns you and you don't like the result, leave the fire alone. It's time that Black people stopped participating in the things that have been put there to destroy them. And the pitfalls are numerous.

On another front, I've heard, and read, that jealousy, *which plagues the Black community*, was taught, and encouraged, amongst the slaves. And I'm sure, that's true. But until we can conquer the problem, as Black people, regardless to where it *came* from, we will not go forward, as a people.

Call it airing our dirty laundry, if you want to, but the dirty laundry is already on the line, for the whole world to see. So, don't think this is any new revelation. Others outside of the Black race have eyes and ears too. And believe it or not, *some of them* want Black people to win this battle too, because they know that, by not carrying our own weight, as citizens, the whole equation is weakened, and the rest of society winds up carrying the non-contributors.

Mind you, I said, *some* of them want us to win. The plain truth is that someone who plies you with drugs and alcohol, and makes a handsome profit from it, is not likely to want to lose you as a customer. So, *you* must break *those* ties, on your own.

And please allow me to point out the fact that most of the liquor store owners doing business in the Black community are not White, but Arabic. Not that it makes much difference, because, until they were bought out by the Arabs, they were largely owned by *Black proprietors*. The fact is, *anyone* will take advantage of you, if you allow them to. So, if you want to blame somebody, put the blame on yourself for taking the bait.

Another point along this line, is the selling of products which are manufactured specifically, for the purpose of denigrating Black people. Such as, malt liquors and other super strength alcoholic beverages sold almost exclusively in Black communities.

Realistic looking guns that are more likely to get Black children killed by police, thinking that the weapon is real. Oh, don't think that I'm excusing, trigger-happy police. What I am saying is, don't let the choice of "toy," be a contributing factor to the reason that something bad happens to your child.

Believe it or not, there are American companies making products and selling them in foreign countries which make all Black people appear to be mindless idiots. The purpose being, to teach others to have little or no respect for Black people also. Often, *before* they come to America, they've already learned to disrespect Black Americans for what they *perceive* us to be, according to what they've been taught about us.

The answer to most of our problems is education, and that's the reason we have been, and are being, steered away from it. In many African American communities, liquor stores are far more accessible than schools.

Schools are dwindling and liquor stores are thriving everywhere, with little or no objection to the fact. Those who would keep you ignorant and poor, are pleased with the silence. I placed the word *ignorant*, before the word *poor* because ignorance, almost *guarantees* poverty. But education eradicates ignorance, thereby lessening the chances of poverty.

Education brings about a spirit of wanting a better life and opens the way to upward mobility. Once you *understand* a situation you start approaching it more smartly. *Ignorance is often the reason for repeating the same mistakes. But being stubborn can also play a big role in holding on to things that you should be rejecting.* "Don't tell me what to do. I'll quit when I'm good and ready!" How many times have we heard that?

Knowledge is built on a system of research. Research helps to eliminate useless elements and ways of doing things, allowing one to constantly add to what they know. Thereby always growing intellectually. But unless you *want knowledge*, you won't *seek it*.

Before we begin trying to get well, we must first realize, and accept, that we are ailing. America, *as a nation*, is sick and ailing. And African Americans are its most seriously ill patients. One big problem is, some of us have yet to accept that many of the causes are self-inflicted.

When one learns a more efficient way of accomplishing something, in the field of education, that knowledge should then be combined with what has been learned previously. From living. The combination of life and education helps to eliminate mistakes and time-wasting, putting the student that much further ahead of where they would be, if they had no base from which to build.

Life plus knowledge produces wisdom. When wisdom is passed on, it increases within the recipient, who builds on it by combining it with his or her own life skills and education.

It is *our responsibility* to add to what has been handed down from our predecessors.

Otherwise it is a waste of knowledge *and* opportunity. Plus, you are leaving those who come after you, at a disadvantage by depriving them of the progress *you could have made* and passed on to them. The cycle of life demands that *we* become better in order to give our offspring a better vantage point from which to begin. And with a history of repression, Black Americans have no time to waste.

One of the cruelest aspects of a legacy of slavery is that, by robbing us of our past, it also *has the potential to rob us of our future. That is, if we let it.* The most important thing in this present time though, is that we *don't rob ourselves*, by allowing ourselves to become complacent. It's like losing all of the information on your hard drive. It's devastating! But you can spend your time worrying about it or you can try to begin all over again from scratch. The sooner you begin, the better.

Since the *literal* shackles have been removed from our people, there are no excuses, or reasons, that we should still be in *mental slavery*. When we get down to business, I think we find that nothing can hold us back like we, ourselves, can.

The *pace* of progress increases with every step of success, because, with success, comes confidence and a hunger for more. The *primer* is that initial achievement. Few things can build up your confidence like accomplishing an important goal, realizing how you did it, and knowing that you can do it again by repeating the steps you took and improving upon them. Since most of us, *Black or White*, don't have a whole lot of material wealth to leave for those coming after us, the least that we can do is try to leave them a wealth of knowledge and try to stimulate their brains.

My thinking is that, "With opportunity, I *must* succeed." When we put our minds to it, we can achieve goals. One of the first steps toward *being* successful, is *seeing yourself as successful*.

If you don't *believe* that you can be a winner, then you probably won't be. And don't rely on anyone else's opinion of you. Have your own *honest* opinion of yourself. If things are where you think they should be, in your life, then continue on that course. But if they are not, don't hesitate to re-evaluate your situation and make the necessary changes.

Don't be afraid to start over from scratch. Testimonies from many people who eventually became successful, tell the story of having to abandon projects which had taken years to accomplish. Whether it was a job position, experiment, or something else that they had poured their heart into, they had to let it go and start over.

The only thing that really matters is being successful. No one cares how long it took you. At the end of the day, *results* are most important. Not how hard it was, or how long it took you. But was it a success?

As a high school student, I attended classes for half of the school day and for the rest of the day I worked at a record store which also carried musical instruments, transistor radios as well as 45 singles and albums. Being located in the heart of downtown, presented a great opportunity for drawing in customers who happened to be just passing by.

Though the windows out front were tiny, the owner found ways to use that space to the best of his advantage. To me, at the time, it just looked like a bunch of junk.

After being there for some time, he decided to let me try my hand at dressing the window. When I was done, he stood back from the window to view it as a potential customer would.

Then, after a long pause, he shook his head and proclaimed a loud, "No! It looks lousy. You have hidden the price tags and obscured our best-selling items." I was instantly furious. "Why did you even ask me to do it?" "Well that's a dumb question. I wanted to see if you knew what you were doing, and you obviously don't!"

This job was a part of the marketing class that I took for the last two years of high school, and I wasn't *about* to walk out. So, I stewed for a couple of days until he said, "You want me to teach you how?", to which I agreed. He began to teach me the "art of dressing a window."

As I got better at it, he would only make a change here and there. Then I realized that it had never really been about the window dressing, but about teaching me things like pride in my work, learning to listen to someone willing to guide me, and patience.

Over those two years, he taught me many things about life and myself. He was a little Jewish man and after he felt that he could talk to me frankly, one day he said to me, "You know… your people never save any money. You spend every dime you get."

I could feel my face, literally burning in anger. How dare he talk to me about *my* people. Out of respect for my elders, which I was brought up to have, I held my peace. But it was *so* hard.

When I had time to reflect on it, I thought, "He's right." I remembered, very well, how my best friend, Herb, and I would do all sorts of odd jobs to have money to be able to buy the latest fashion trend. Willing to spend our hard-earned money, just to look good. And although I'm still not as frugal as I would like to be, when I start to spend too heavily, I can hear the words of Mr. Jerry Solomon saying, "Your people never save any money. You spend every dime you get." And I pull back on the spending.

The last day that I worked there, I remember him standing there looking me in the face, arms folded and saying, "I know you didn't like me when you first started working here. I know, I know. But you've been a great student. And I'm a pretty good teacher. When you think about me, think about the good stuff. If you miss me, *and you will*, stop in and say 'hi' sometime. Now get outta here."

With a handshake and a smile, we said goodbye. Years later, when I stopped by to say hello, the store had changed locations and he had passed away. But I still hear that voice in my head, at the right moments.

While, at first, I thought of Mr. Solomon as only the man that I worked for, years later I began to recognize the fact that he was, *indeed*, one of my teachers. And in a big way. While the others were teaching me curriculum, he was teaching me life. And they are both necessary.

One of the things that made Mr. Berry Gordy Jr. successful with Motown Records was the *vision* that he had. He envisioned Motown's music being "the sound of young America." *All*, of young America.

And that's what it became. Not just young *Black* America. He began with an idea and put the necessary steps in motion. He enlisted the best talent that he could find to write, record, and produce music that would appeal to a wide variety of people. It sounds much simpler than it was.

To begin with, he had to compete with already established companies who had top-notch professionals in every department. Writers (musical and lyrical), session musicians, producers, engineers. You name it, they had it. And top that off with rich production and promotional budgets. These facts alone, could be enough to give some people a huge complex.

But that is what separates the winners and losers. One thing to take note of here is that winners have a vision *and* a plan. *In order to have a plan, some planning must be done beforehand.*

Part of Mr. Gordy's plan was to deliver to his perceived audiences, short and interesting stories in the form of records. One of his greatest assets in the lyrical and melodic department was Mr. William "Smokey" Robinson.

The stories that Smokey wrote in his songs helped to bring "Rhythm and Blues" music to another level of sophistication. If he had listened to critics, they would probably have advised him to simplify the lyrics, but instead he educated the listener by bringing them along on *his journey*.

Songs like, "My Girl", which helped to make the vocal group, The Temptations, a household name. Eddie Holland, Lamont Dozier, and Brian Holland under the songwriting and production team Holland Dozier Holland, added to the sophistication by penning hit after hit for the Supremes, which featured lead singer Ms. Diana Ross.

Shortly thereafter, Motown took the world by storm, establishing themselves as *the* recording company that everyone tried to measure up to. Creating music that is still in the forefront of the music industry after all these years. Putting Detroit on the map with the new nickname, "Motown", and highlighting the vast array of talented people who resided in Detroit, Michigan.

You might say, "What's in a name?" First of all, a name can draw people to you or make them ridicule you. So, a name can determine whether you are received or rejected right from the start.

Before Motown Records, Black popular music was in what was called the Doowop era. During which they sang songs that, for the most part, were lacking in meaningful content. Having names like birds, cars, and other names which made them sound silly, in many cases. I assume this was to be more accepted and less offensive to White audiences.

Ironically, the group with the most offensive name, "The Ink Spots", had some of the most intellectually appealing songs. I guess the name took away the threat of being labeled as too uppity.

Motown groups, without making it so obvious, changed all of that. The songs had substance, or they didn't pass quality inspection. A vote of approval by a board deemed as "quality control" had to be met before *any* single was released.

And the names were ones the artists could be proud of, like The Temptations. Which would probably, because of sounding "desirable", have been too uppity, for five Black guys in the past. The Supremes, meaning the very best. The Miracles, which Motown, itself, was. Edwin Starr with *two* r's. Motown made bold statements and backed them up. Claiming to be the best, and by all accounts, *being* the best.

No matter who tells you, "you can't", if you tell yourself that you can, *and believe it*, success can be yours. Just be prepared to work hard to make your vision a reality. Remember you will need a vision *and* a plan. I truly believe that *defeat* begins in the mind the same as *success* does.

I know that there has to be losers in order to have winners, but if you're going to have any real chance of winning, you must approach the situation realistically and with confidence. If it is something that could have been prepared for, then you should have worked as hard as you could at preparing, in order to be confident that you *know* what you are doing.

There is no one who can destroy your hopes and chances like *you* can. By allowing doubt a space in your mind, you can do more damage to *yourself* than a whole *team* of detractors. By the same token, with a confident mindset, the hardest part of the job is already accomplished.

But as I stated previously, in order to be confident, you must prepare *before* the moment of truth. I've heard people make statements like, "I'm going to get inside of their head." That can only happen to a person who is unprepared or lacking in confidence. A person who is confident in the true sense of the word, is *prepared* because *preparation gave them* their confidence.

There *is* such a thing as "false confidence", which is a type of cockiness. Being bold, without being qualified, having done nothing to warrant that attitude. Like taking an unknown journey without relying on a roadmap, because you feel you're smart enough to do it on instinct. That's false confidence, especially when compared to a person who *utilizes* the roadmap. You're setting *yourself* up for failure. "Who put you in this foolish predicament?" "Me."

Many are the reasons for feeling not good enough. Things like being poor, uneducated, weak (physically or mentally; or both), discrimination (of various types), or physically handicapped. But not even one of these is a good enough reason to *keep you feeling not good enough.*

Most of us start out with some apprehension as we begin our journey through life. Some are concerned with their own state of affairs. Some are more concerned with other peoples' state of affairs than their own. It could be for good reasons or bad. For wanting to help *or* wanting to control. And some are just not concerned about any state of affairs at all.

I have noticed that ignorance (not knowing) and lack of education can give people a tremendous chip on their shoulders. A real inferiority complex. "What are you saying, I'm stupid?!" "You think you know everything!"

Feelings of inadequacy *hatched and nurtured*, all by themselves. They know that you know something that they don't know, but their own feeling of being not good enough won't allow them to get past the embarrassment of needing to reach out for help. So, they blame others for their shortcomings and suffer under their self-inflicted pain of ignorance.

There is a lot of that going on among people in general. In fact, this is the basis of many of the arguments that result in violent assaults among family members and people who are known to each other. Pettiness is causing some people to lash out at those who might point out their faults or, without malicious intent, correct something that they have said or done.

The smart people take advice *or correction* and keep it moving. That's how they *got* smart. *By trading and compiling information.* My grandmother used to say, "A person who knows everything is full and can't hold anything else." It took me a while to realize that she was being sarcastic. What she meant was, "I'm not going to waste my time, trying to teach a bull-headed person who thinks they already know everything."

To the person who wants to move forward, life is about revelations, adaptations, and motivation. Revelations that have come to you by way of interaction and association with others and by paying attention to life, in general.

After you have received *certain* revelations, there is a need to adapt to them by letting go of old ideas and embracing new ones that have been identified as the truth. *As it applies to you.*

Once you can see that things are not what you might have thought they were previously, don't be reluctant to make the necessary adjustments. Keeping only those old ideas which are certain to compliment the new ones. There is an art in knowing what to throw away and what to keep. Motivation comes naturally when everything lines up properly, because you will automatically want to capitalize on the success of your achievements up to this point. Enjoying the fruits of your labor.

Customary is a big part of the American vocabulary. Since customs (the way we do things) have played such an important role in keeping things the way they are in America, you can expect to hear the phrase, "No, that's not customary", anytime someone expresses a desire for change. As a Black person, I'm tired of looking around and seeing so many customary reminders of slavery.

I believe that there is something seriously wrong with anyone who would even *want* to hold on to sentiments of slavery. So, to fight to preserve the statues and marketplaces where slavery took place, around the country, because they're historic, is just plain evil.

Yet they get offended when they hear the phrase, "Black lives matter." And retort by saying, "All lives matter," or "Blue lives matter." I honestly believe that everyone knows that the, "Black lives matter," phrase *is* saying that Black people are disproportionately being killed by police, as if our lives don't matter. So, in that respect, I consider those who take offense to be an enemy of Black people.

There is no right or wrong time or place to call attention to the mistreatment of a people, or an individual, for that matter. For that reason, I have the utmost respect for Colin Kaepernick, whom, while being at the top of his game, making millions playing football, risked it all, to take a stand against the brutal annihilation of his, and my, people. For someone to say he was wrong, or his timing was off, is showing a certain callousness toward the endangerment of Black lives.

Because of having lived in poverty, and not ever wanting to find ourselves there again, some of us begin to worship money, and put, "making money", before our very own wellbeing, and definitely, before the wellbeing of others. "That ain't got nothing to do with me. Let that fool go on and do whatever he wants to." While the the streets are being littered with our peoples' blood.

I've got time for the cause. If I'm an endangered species, but I'm the richest, most beautiful creature in the jungle, what difference will it make if they've killed off all of my kind and I'm the last, richest, and most beautiful and now in the crosshairs of the annihilator? I am just a *dead*, rich, beautiful creature who trusted in vanity and money.

CHAPTER 4

A Way Out

One thing that is discussed, seriously, among African Americans in the poor communities, which is most of them, is "getting out." Meaning, pulling themselves up out of poverty. There are many ways in which this is pursued, but one of the main attempts is through the avenue of sports. Children are often encouraged by their parents from the first sign of any athleticism, to be "the next Michael Jordon or Lebron James."

I believe this often happens without much thought given to the fact that there is a limited amount of positions in professional sports. So there really is not enough room to accommodate *all* of the aspiring *and qualified* athletes.

So many potentially great athletes get left high and dry. Literally. High, because they often turn to drugs or alcohol, or both. Dry, in the sense that they sometimes become bitter and angry at the world. When you realize that you could perform at the level of the top players in a professional sport, and don't get the chance, it's bound to affect your mind, in some way.

And few people handle this well. In my opinion, a person, regardless of what they are gifted in, should first pursue the scholastic road to success. If they are scholastically inclined. That is, if they have the mental skills and aptitude for higher learning.

Not everyone does, but there are other areas, like skilled labor (working with your hands) and crafts, mechanics, or anything else which requires a skill. That is, so they will have something to, " fall back on," as my father used to say. The problem is that when most young people are aspiring to professional sports, because the competition is so intense, they feel that they can't afford to do anything but practice for their future spot on a professional team. Not even allowing themselves to consider the *possibility* of not "making it."

Someone needs to remind them before it comes down to "not making it," that the reality is; there are only so many new positions filled every year because most of the players remain on the roster for some years, if they are still performing at the required level. Getting injured before or shortly after getting signed could also put an end to their career.

We need to get away from that, "all or nothing", way of thinking. As we older folks know, there is a *lot* between *all* and *nothing*. Just because you don't have it all, doesn't mean you have to be stuck with nothing.

I am left to wonder if sometimes the reason these young people are not warned is because parents and others around them, are not seeing the picture clearly themselves. Anticipating these athletes as being *their* way out, as well. That's understandable since they might have invested much of their time and money into the *future star*. But everyone needs to keep in mind that it's a *potential star*. As many of those who were left out, know, you can be great and still not make it, for a lot of reasons.

One of the saddest and most disappointing things about professional sports is the number of athletes who make millions of dollars and fail to hold on to it or invest it properly and wind up broke. This is the case for most retired athletes. And the vast majority of these are African American.

On the other hand, some African American athletes have retired and done very well. Some have not retired but it appears that they have their business ends together.

Some of the most successful ones are Tiger Woods, Michael Jordan, Serena and Venus Williams, Lebron James, and Ervin "Magic" Johnson. I know that wisdom says, "Don't hire family members and close friends." But Lebron is doing quite well with his team of personal African American friends working closely with him, in a business capacity.

A more recent door which has opened to Black athletes is the game of hockey. Young Black players have begun to dominate the sport of hockey since being allowed to play in the National Hockey League. There was a time when only, the great goalie, Grant Fuhr, was allowed in the game. But being a goalie, he wore a mask, which was probably less offensive to the mostly White fans.

Another way out has always been by way of music. But, the same as sports, the roster is never as open as expected and the pitfalls are many. Although music, unless it's hip hop, has fallen off, as a lucrative commodity, the industry would have us believe that everything is still, "on and popping." One sure indication that revenues from music have declined, is the type of contract being offered to potential artists these days. The contract is called a 360.

What the new contract requires, is the same things that they have always required, plus a percentage of your concert revenue and also a percentage of your merchandise sales (tee shirts, posters, etc.). The main reason is, people are not buying cd's, USB's or any other hard forms of music anymore.

And the music that they *are* buying by way of downloads is pretty much being given away through streams. Ask yourself, when was the last time you bought a cd? You are not alone. That's why cd's are being phased out. They are not selling.

African American producers and artists who were fortunate enough to do well when R&B was hot in recent years, were blessed to have a man that they could go to, once they started collecting their money. Or when they needed to structure their business and financial affairs. His name is Mr. Clarence Avant. He was an executive in the music industry, in different capacities, for many years. I have a feeling though, that he's aided and touched many lives in different professions throughout the African American community. Sir, you are indeed a treasure.

CHAPTER 5

Blurry Separation Lines

Since the beginning of time, people have shared, borrowed, or *stolen* ideas from others, in order to expand upon that knowledge with ideas of their own. Certainly, much of the knowledge available to the modern world has been compiled and archived by our predecessors.

Leaving us with great positioning from which to start our quests for higher learning and to build upon. For instance, the reason that we know which existing plants and medicines can cure certain sicknesses is because that information has been compiled and passed on, from the past, for someone else to use, and hopefully, improve upon.

On the other hand, many animals, *and people*, have died or been sacrificed in the name of such progress. How do we know that a particular plant is poisonous? Because another living creature either got sick or died to prove it. The premise that a *good idea* can become a *better one* is what has kept the world constantly evolving since the beginning of time.

Living in an unfamiliar environment tends to bring out the innovative spirit in people. It's called survival. It becomes necessary to absorb the ways of the people with whom you co-exist, the ones who were there first, because their ways have already been proven. In the case of America, that would be the Native tribes of the First Nations.

Of course, many of the European customs, and much of their culture, was forced upon the Natives *and* Africans, as a way of bringing them under subjection and asserting *their* control and dominance over them. And, also because they felt that they were more *civilized* than the others, which they reminded them of, on a regular basis. "Heathens" and "barbarians" were the terms often used to describe those of non-European backgrounds. Some of those spoken of in such terms even began to adopt the ways of the Europeans, trying to fit in, or maybe to be thought of as less of a threat.

The assimilation took place in many different forms. Sometime after slavery Black women began to "straighten" their hair, by pressing it out with something called a "hot comb". Which was a piece of metal, heated up, with teeth cut into it, for pulling through the coarse texture of Black hair to thin it out and make it appear more like "White peoples' hair."

This was such a phenomenon that a Black entrepreneur by the name of Madame C.J. Walker became the first wealthy Black woman in America by selling products related to Black people seeking a Whiter look. By straightening their hair and adopting what they considered to be a European style.

Not too long after that, some Black *men* decided to join the fray and started to "process" their own hair in a most un-safe way, by using a mixture of lye and potatoes which made their hair straighter. Immediately products were manufactured to support this style, as well. Of course, no one admitted that they were trying to be someone other than their natural self. It just "looked" good.

As the trends have never stopped, but increased, I have heard Black women with dyed blond hair state that, "I look better with this color of hair than White women do." Who's to argue the point? After all, isn't beauty in the eyes of the beholder?

For years, some White people have criticized, Black people for having "big noses", "thick lips", "dark skin", and large backsides. In recent years many White people, mostly females, have been guilty of adding some of these same characteristics, through surgery and tanning, to their own bodies. And with the same attitude of the Black women who said, "I look better in this than *they* do."

A recent trend is that it's desirable for women to have a bigger backside, because that is what many men are looking for in a woman. Since many Black women have been endowed with that, naturally, this is nothing new to them. As most Black men have always loved that in Black women. The new thing is that the lips, big back sides, and darker skin are now being "explored" by *White* women.

At the same time, some Black people are lightening their skin color through scientific methods. Having their noses surgically slimmed down, wearing colored contact lenses, (of a shade not natural for Black people) having their lips thinned and *basically rejecting their Blackness*. Sounds like more of a love affair with the opposite race going on here than people care to admit to. And it's flowing in both directions.

There is a whole industry that is providing hair for women to weave into their existing hair to make a fuller, longer head of hair. With White women claiming that Black women are trying to look like them and Black women complaining that White women are getting "butt enhancements" to try to look like them. Once again, a mutual admiration is going on that no one wants to admit to.

"Pop culture", meaning Popular culture, has dictated that, "If it feels and looks good on you, that is all that matters." The "bling" effect has taken precedence over substance. To be honest, tastes in fashion, sports, and music, often bring people of different races together in a strange kind of way.

For instance, sports have attained almost a type of religious reverence in America. Whereby, people of different races who would not otherwise communicate with each other, can be found passionately discussing the wins or losses of their favorite team, with the very same people that they *disdain* under other circumstances.

Sports have such a powerful influence among Americans, that people will wear the jersey, tennis shoes, hats, of their favorite athletes even though they dislike people of that particular race, usually the Black race. It is because, probably without realizing it, for a short period, out of their lives, they have laid aside their differences and embraced something that they like about a person or persons from that group.

When their passion of the moment for that game, playoff, or athlete subsides, then it's back to normal. No friendly communication or association. Sometimes for fear their friends might see them discussing something other than sports and think they might be associating for reasons other than the *"allowed"* common interest in sports. This is often taking place in a work environment. Which for many Whites and Blacks, is the only time *any* type of interaction takes place between them.

Music is another area of "cross pollination" between the Black and White races. There are sounds which we relate to as being either White or Black. So much so that when we hear a person of the one race sounding like a person of the opposite race, we tend to feel like they're "sounding Black" or "sounding White".

The way a story is told, depends on who is telling it. For this reason, there have been a lot of disagreements between Blacks and Whites about who contributed the most to making America what it has become.

Over the years Black people have laid claim to originating many cultural developments, that are thought of as indigenous to America.

Things such as Jazz and Blues music. It helps Black pride to be able to say, "Without us America would be a very boring place." But the truth is, this country is a melting pot. With cultural contributions flowing from so many directions that it's hard to keep up with whom to attribute them to.

The Africans brought dance, so did the Europeans, albeit different styles. One makes fun of the other, but the truth is they have *borrowed from each other,* in so many ways. The Africans brought rhythm and the Europeans brought melody. When the melodies and rhythms came together, they produced the origins of blues, and eventually jazz, within the Black community, and later, country music from within the White community.

There is a saying that states, "What comes from the heart, reaches the heart." And, so it is with music. In many instances, music has been the bridge which has brought people together and it has also been the glue which has *kept* them together in a kind of loose manner.

You can find people from all walks of life, different races, ethnic backgrounds, who love the same types of music. An avowed racist can love the music made by the people whom they claim to hate. So, in that respect, it is no surprise that music has cross pollinated between the races and even countries.

Blues music which originated out of Black poverty and misery has come to be all but abandoned, by many African Americans, for being contrary to their Christian beliefs and because of the stigma of poverty and slavery associated with it. But it has been embraced by many White Americans with open arms. With a large majority claiming Blues as their favorite genre of music altogether. Sometimes I wonder if they love it for the same reason that some Blacks dislike it. For the sake of keeping the slave/sharecropper syndrome alive. Or if they love it for the "soulfulness" of it.

Contrary to the norm, Jimi Hendrix, an African American, was a major player and unprecedented guitar virtuoso in the field of Rock music, which is mostly thought of as White music. Many White and Black people share an open love for Hendrix's music. The significance of this is, White people *accepting* a Black man playing "their" music and Black people *approving* of a Black man playing "White peoples' music."

Everything else aside, he was so *good* at what he did that he was undeniable. So was Elvis Presley, a White man who came out singing Black music and was soon accepted by music fans across the board.

At the same time though, Elvis put the country in an uproar. Many White people who were not overwhelmed by his music were put off by him recording the very music that they had tried to suppress in order not to give the so-called Negro a national voice.

While many of Elvis' White critics complained about his gyrating hips, it was really about him promoting the "Black sound." But then someone recognized the fact that, here was a White man who sounded *close enough* to the Black sound, *without being Black*. Having a look that was not bad on the eyes and singing like that, they could market him to White audiences and make a ton of money. His manager, "The Colonel" did just that. And the rest, as they say, is history.

Once again, love overruled hatred and not only did Elvis succeed, but paved the way and created acceptance for other artists like himself, both Black and White. Still though, some Blacks criticized him for "stealing" Black music and, as previously stated some Whites criticized him for legitimizing it. The general opinion, though, is that he broke down some barriers, for himself and others, and gave us good music at the same time.

White America's biggest, and most original, musical contribution is, unquestionably, country music. And like most original forms of American music it has gained worldwide fan acceptance and appreciation. Considered the folk music of the mostly poor and rural White southerners, country music is as White as American music gets. And the love of it is international.

Yet a Black man, with a heart for Country music, was not only accepted, *but embraced* by Country music lovers everywhere. I speak of none other than Mr. Charley Pride who rode the wave of success in Country music for longer than a lot of successful *White* country artists.

He was accepted not as a novelty, *that would never have worked,* but as one whose *heart and soul* were country. But here again, *he was good at it.* Even with all of her hang-ups, America accepts greatness, no matter where it comes from.

I believe that to be the *true* American spirit. No matter how we lie and deny it, our actions speak differently. Be the very best and there will be a place for you. This is debatable but has proven *true* in many cases.

The following is an article about a documentary, *American Masters - Charley Pride: I'm Just Me*, telling the story of how Charlie Pride met Faron Young, who was the man he had to be accepted by, in order to be thought of as a *legitimate* country singer. As told by Lloyd Green, Mr. Pride's longtime steel guitarist: Green continued, "I'm from Mobile, Alabama, and you've got to consider the era of [the 1960s]. Charley was so disarming, being able to have a great sense of humor about the color barrier at that time. I think that's one of the major points in Charley's favor, that he never let people get to him by using the color thing against him. He was thoughtful about those things, but he never had any anger or animosity.

We were in the studio once when Faron Young burst in, and just stood there glaring up at Charley with his hands on his hips. No one would say a word, so... he grabbed Charley and kissed him on the lips, saying, 'I love you, Charley Pride.' It was an epiphanous moment because once he did that, Nashville accepted Charley. Faron Young could cause a lot of problems back then, and sometimes did, so once he accepted Charley everyone else kind of had to, too."

The previous article was taken from a Billboard magazine review of the PBS documentary, American Masters - Charley Pride: I'm Just Me. *Feb.2019, The article was written by Isaac Weeks, dated 02/22/2019. Film Directed by Barbara J. Hall.*

Many Black people at the time felt that Charlie must be out of his mind to be singing country songs and hanging out with White people at a time when we were struggling against the racist machine of segregation. Then most of us began to realize that he was doing his part to break down the barrier in another way. Years later, while attending a Rick James recording session with a friend of mine, the engineer informed us that he was a cousin to Charlie Pride and joked that if we told anyone that he would have to "get us." Of course, he was proud of him or he never would have mentioned it.

Who wouldn't be proud of a man who accomplished so many unbelievable feats. In a 21 year recording career he had 52 top-10 hit records on the Billboard Hot Country Songs chart. Out of those 52, 30 of them went to #1.

Tiger Woods (golf), Serena Williams, and Venus Williams (tennis), are also, examples of greatness transcending racism. The sports that they have dominated were once considered to be for Whites only.

Even though they have risen through the ranks in their respective sports, it has not been done without encountering some racism. But it takes greatness to reach as far as they have, and to be perfectly honest, there was a time when no matter how good they were, they would still not have gotten the chance to participate. In that respect, I can truly say that America has changed, but still has a long way to go.

I can't help but believe that most of America, Native, White, Black, Hispanic, Asian and Arabic are sick of racism. It affects us all in one way or another. Often getting in the way of progress. We are all Americans and most of us are here to stay so we might as well introduce ourselves, roll up our sleeves and begin to make America a great place *for everyone* to be.

I'm not too sure if it's because this is America, and we are accustomed to being divided along racial lines, or if we really do just have different natural styles and ways of doing things. But I believe that a lot of our problems stem from *pointing out* our differences as opposed to just *accepting* them.

After living among each other for so many years, Blacks and Whites have begun to assimilate into a more homogenous existence. Despite their distrust for one another.

One of the problems with enslaving a people in such large numbers, as Blacks in America, it becomes harder to control them. And when the slaves have been freed, learning to co-exist with them presents another problem. After the treatment that the slaves received, can we trust them not to retaliate? How do they *really* feel about us? Where do we *put* them?

Unless they had a way of taking the Africans *back* to Africa, the Europeans had to learn to co-exist with them. The first thing to be established was, that, the two parties would live in separate communities and not associate on a social level. Black people would live in the least desired parts of whatever city, town, or rural area they resided in, usually close to railroad tracks. Probably for easy deployment of troops or militia in case of an uprising.

Trying to make people live in communities, separated by invisible boundaries, has proven to be unenforceable, except by laws. Over the years these laws, which were in existence, have been struck down as unconstitutional. This has resulted in Black people moving into formerly all -White neighborhoods, which has caused unrest and drawn intimidation from some of those living in these neighborhoods, who are against any type of Black and White integration.

Sometimes entire neighborhoods are abandoned, by Whites who refuse to live among Blacks and, sometimes *other* non-Whites. By the same token, there are some White people who will not live among certain other *White people* because they feel their standards are not high enough.

The term, "trailer trash" is a term coined by Whites, to describe White people who live in trailer parks, but has also come to be used to describe what they consider to be, "low level" Whites not necessarily living in trailer parks, just not up to *their standards*. "White trash," is another of those terms used by Whites who feel that they are personally in a higher class.

For those who feel this way, they would probably still consider these White people to be in a *slightly* higher category than Black people, yet undesirable to be around. If not for the *suffering* caused by these stereotypes, it could be comical. All of these groups of people interacting in so many ways, yet looking down on, or looking up to someone just because of a perceived social status or color.

No matter what the social level of a person's status is, most of us are trying to obtain the same objectives: Good health, feeding and clothing our household, maintaining a place of residency, holding down a job, and being responsible citizens.

There are those, who have been brainwashed into thinking that this kind of mindset couldn't *possibly* apply to Black people. And believe it or not, *some* who think this way are Black themselves. Looking down on other Black people and feeling like they are better. Believing that because *they* have achieved a higher standard of living, anyone else should be able to do the same, with hard work and determination. *Which isn't always true.*

Because Black people, are so often impressed by White people who, speak and act " Black", and seem to show a certain amount of knowledge about Black culture, our race has been exploited from within and without. Examples can be found in music, fashion, movies, and everyday life. How often have you heard someone speaking and without seeing their face, assumed that they were Black, when upon seeing their faces, finding that they were indeed White or not Black?

This has become a problem for some people of the White race, who feel that other White people are adopting Black culture as *their own*. Sometimes causing more dislike for Blacks, as if to say, "Look what you've done! Got these people acting like you." Laws, while being put in place to prevent the mixing of cultures can only go so far in achieving what they were meant to. People are just people and they are attracted to what appeals to them personally.

The mentality is that, if it *works for me* and satisfies my taste, then it's *okay for me*. Regardless of where it came from. Whether it be fashion, music, literature, or any other form of culture, it becomes a matter of taste. If we like or love something, it doesn't matter where it came from. When people are living among each other and having a chance to see and hear the things that capture their imaginations, it's going to be reflected in their lifestyles. Crossing culture lines is inevitable in *any* social situation. In America and everywhere else around the world, it seems to be a human trait.

Examples of acting, "conveniently Black" are White recording artists who start out using the Black sound, sometimes managed and produced by someone Black. Black people who are always willing to show love to a White person displaying Black traits, support the artist right out of the box.

Then when they "cross-over" to a White audience and don't need the Black support anymore, their Black fans are left feeling used and betrayed. With the number of times it has happened, they should have seen it coming. I can think of at least three females and one male artist who have done just that.

The insult which is considered most offensive is when the White artists cross-over from Black audiences to White ones, they choose to play rock music, which is considered White music. That is the ultimate "burn", because then it becomes *obvious* that the Black audience has been used as a steppingstone. To those who would take offense toward me labeling things as Black and White, I didn't invent any of this, it is already the way things are. I'm just narrating according to what is already there. Before things change, we have to admit that something is wrong. Things won't change themselves we must do it.

The re-appropriation of Black culture has been going on for so long and has become so widespread that even some younger generations of *Black people* are unaware that many things which are accepted by the general public as just being "American" originated in the Black community. Which is not to say that it's a bad thing, because anything that brings us closer together, is good in some way. It's just that the more we know about our contributions the more it can bring a sense of pride, confidence, and belonging.

Some Black people have been left so ashamed by the legacy of slavery that they only allow themselves to be proud of their Blackness when it is spoken of in terms of Black people being kings and queens back in Africa. But never in a "right now" situation. They deny their affinity to other Black people around them, except when it's "cool" to be Black. The truth is, not *all* Africans were kings and queens, although that is *a part* of the heritage of the African continent.

   Another thing that a lot of people are unaware of is that, even while being enslaved in this country, some of our ancestors were creating and inventing things that they were never credited for because their inventions and ideas were registered in White peoples' names. Usually the plantation owner. We, (Black people) have much to be proud of, if we would study our *true* history. And it's there for us, but once again, somebody hid it in a book. And in our case, hid the book.

"Where Anything Goes; Anything Grows"

CHAPTER 6

A New Normal

A society which adheres to morality is more likely to obey the laws of the land, as opposed to an *immoral* society. By now, many of us are familiar with the post war picture of the young lady and the sailor kissing in Times Square, while celebrating the end of World War II. At first glance, it looks harmless, but *before the war*, that type of behavior would less likely have been accepted in most parts of America. I've read the story behind the picture and it states that those two people were complete strangers to each other.

In today's America, many people reading this will take offence to the fact that I would even insinuate that such behavior was wrong, *in any way*. It was just a simple celebration of the end of a war which lasted too long and consumed too many precious lives. "What's wrong with a celebration?" It depends on who you are claiming to be and the *nature* of the celebration.

America has claimed Puritan values and morals from its beginning. *But it was a lie, even then*. To enslave a whole race of people, or *anyone* for that matter, is *immoral*. Just as brutalizing a nation of people, in order to take their land, is immoral.

But that's how America *became* America. By brute force. Then, after realizing that these people whom they had enslaved and brutalized would have to coexist with them, they made some concessions. But with restrictions which would keep the power in the hands of the "ruling class".

World War II, for America, consisted of many hard-fought battles, which at times, seemed like America might not win the war. But we did. And the main reason the war was won was because of the American citizens' (military and civilian) resilience and solidarity, in our war effort.

The victory can be claimed by people from every race and community in America. European Americans, African Americans, Native Americans, Asian Americans, Hispanic Americans, and even Inuit Americans.

That is the depth of our war effort. After the war was won, it gave us cause to celebrate. During the celebration, some things were allowed to happen that were unacceptable before the war but gained acceptance and are even more widely accepted today.

Sex and alcohol flowed much more loosely and led to a demoralization of this country that still haunts us today. I'm not suggesting that before the war, no one had illicit sex or drank alcohol.

What I am saying is, our attitude toward them both became lax. In a way which has cost us dearly in our output and productivity. Many workplaces now include drug addiction and alcohol abuse departments for treating their employees. Alcohol consumption has reached such a level of tolerance that, although it is destroying lives, it has been elevated to a status of being thought of as, almost glamorous to be seen with a drink in hand.

In fact, most ads and commercials for alcoholic beverages are using *sex to sell their products*. Be it a beautiful woman, a nice car, or the outright suggestion that drinking makes you more appealing to the opposite sex. Giving the viewer the impression that it's sexy and glamorous to drink alcohol. That depending on your choice of drink, you can meet the guy, or girl, of your dreams.

The celebration has lasted far too long and has produced a society which seems to only want to celebrate *and not do much else*. As a country, we're shooting ourselves in the foot, for a profit. If it brings in the money, then we're all for it. Capitalism at its finest. Sell enough of something and you can *be* somebody. Doesn't matter much, what it is you're selling or whom it's hurting.

You're a smart "businessperson" if you're turning a profit. The "suckers", the ones being taken advantage of, on the lower level, are always the poorest of any society. In America that includes some poor Whites, poor Hispanics, poor Native peoples, and poor Blacks. Which, let's face it, is *the majority of* Black, Native, and Hispanic people. Probably Whites too. With the *percentage* being higher in the non-White races though.

It really is heartbreaking to see what is happening to this country, right before our eyes. And there seems to be, not much that we can do about it. The drugs, the careless sex, the killing, and just basic demoralization are taking us down at breakneck speed. And it's all happening so seemingly free and unrestricted.

One of the main reasons for the widespread drug and alcohol dependency is hopelessness. People are trying to escape from their realities, their present circumstances of being in dire need. With no solution, or way out, in sight. All too often their perception of what success is, has been delivered from a medium that was designed just for that purpose. *To show us what success looks like, then make it unattainable, by putting stumbling blocks in our way. Drugs and alcohol being the main obstacles.*

You might say, "Nobody is making people buy the drugs or alcohol." With that being true. The granting of liquor licenses is disproportionately awarded to merchants selling alcohol in the poorest of communities. Making it readily available and strongly pushing it, through commercials (radio and television), billboards and other advertisement mediums.

The former mayor of the city of Detroit, Michigan, Kwame Kilpatrick, once proposed a bylaw to greatly limit the number of licenses given to liquor stores in his city, for obvious reasons. The backlash was very strong coming from local storeowners, who reminded him, "We're providing a large portion of your tax base." And those addicted to readily available alcohol, claimed, "They're providing a service to the community. So, leave them alone." And since not enough people would stand with him, his idea had to be abandoned. To the detriment of the city.

And when the question arises, "Where are the *drugs* coming from," no one seems to know. Except, everyone knows poor people don't possess any means for bringing them into the country. Why is all of this allowed to happen? How can the nation's poorest people be set upon by those who are benefiting strictly from taking advantage of them and no one does anything about it? Simply because there are two separate societies operating in America. The wealthy and the non-wealthy. The former, wants to *keep* it that way.

As we all know, wealth means control. When money controls the game, anything goes. *In the name of making money.* So, in that respect, more wealth for the wealthy, means less of everything for the rest of us. Fewer rights for the masses, due to less control, more starving people because of less money to spare for feeding the hungry. It's a pretty dim outlook, and appearing dimmer, as time goes by.

With domestic terrorism being more of a real threat than ever before, it gives the authorities the right to extend their reach further into our private lives, in the name of preventing some of the citizenry from committing subversive acts. Which to a certain degree, looks necessary, in light of seeming threats coming from so many directions.

But we need to question, how much of it is for our protection, and how much is for limiting our rights for the sake of controlling us. What better way to put you under subjection, than do it under the guise of "doing it for your protection." Before you know it, *the ones who are supposed to be protecting you, could be controlling you.*

The biggest war being fought, by American citizens, presently, is the war for our rights as citizens. Freedom, as we've known it, is being taken away through legalities that are being pushed through right under our noses.

Federal, state, and local governments are coming up with new laws, designed to limit our rights. Constantly. And all the while people are allowed, *if not encouraged*, to forego becoming formerly educated.

It's easier to *control* an *uneducated people*. If you don't want to go to school, no one's forcing you to, anymore. Schools are closing at an alarming rate and penal institutions are being built, just as quickly, to house an uneducated, ignorant society, that is being fostered by the failure to bring them along on the journey to prosperity. But it (prosperity) was never, really intended for *everyone*, in the first place. It was only intended for you to *believe* that it was for everyone.

If the hand had been tipped too soon, then you might have realized the game was rigged, and not have played along with it. But, because they let you *think* that you had a chance to win, *and were in the game,* you marched on, oblivious to what the long-term plan was. You thought that the American dream belonged to everyone. You were encouraged to buy homes, cars, and other trinkets which proved that you were a part of that dream. *Or so you thought.*

Then one day the bottom suddenly fell out. What was the American dream for some, became the American nightmare for others. Some of the disenfranchised of the White race, suddenly realized that they were no better off, financially, than their Black counterparts. But those in control, always find a way to keep the division alive, among the poor, by perpetuating racism. And finding enough people, all too willing to take the bait.

Let's be realistic though. Although ignorance is subtly *and* overtly *promoted* to the poor, especially poor Black people, it doesn't have to be accepted. Just because someone wishes me to be ignorant, even to the point of putting obstacles in my way, doesn't mean I can't go around them. In fact, in *my* mind, I *must* go around them.

The responsibility for my progress, or *lack of progress* in my life, is ultimately, my own. I'll get as far as I can take myself, by the knowledge that I achieve, coupled with how hard I work and apply it. Not by how far someone else *allows* me reach. You can limit me for only so long. The poor, both White *and* Black, have been unwittingly pitted against each other, in order to keep them from ever uniting to fight a common cause, which is an oppressive system, taking advantage of *all* parties.

While some groups only concern themselves with keeping the *races* from mixing, there is another group of higher-ranking individuals who are concerned with doing whatever it takes to prevent collective thinking among the masses of people in this country. While, *stoking the fires of separation* also. That is how they are allowed to continue controlling us.

Keeping the majority of people divided, gives them the advantage of sewing discord among the fragments of people, making it easier to control the whole group. Without them even realizing that they are *being* controlled. If the fragments (divided people) became one collective and began to communicate among themselves, eyes would be opened, and the focus might then be turned toward the manipulators.

In a democratic society, just like any other, there *has to* be order and hierarchy for things to run smoothly. And not everyone can be in control at the same time. Most importantly though, the citizenship needs to be able to trust that their country is in the hands of people who have their best interest at heart. It seems that somewhere along the way, our leaders felt that giving in to the peoples' desires to live immorally, would keep them preoccupied, and satisfied, while the leaders had their way with running the country however they saw fit.

The result is a country with decaying morals and not much, in the way of patriotism, holding things together. Add to this, the racial tension in America and you have a very volatile mix. There was a time when a few words from a respected government official or a trusted leader could be enough to soothe the minds of a country in need of direction. However, that is seldom the case anymore because of the lack of trusted community leaders. And respected government officials are getting harder to find.

When people feel that they have been *mis-directed* it makes it that much harder to trust *anyone*. Because we have always made such an easy target, non-Whites are often focused on as *the reason* for the current state of affairs and used as a diversion, when the real problem lies with the system that is controlling *all of us*.

For a while, it seemed like we were on the right track. Black people saw legislation passed which laid out the rights to certain freedoms that we had never experienced in America. Women gained rights that had been previously denied them also. There was a sigh of relief and a sense of gain, felt by all. But remember, *"The true value of freedom lies in what you do with it."*

As in the case of Black America, sometimes the struggle can be so hard that, after it's over, you just want to "relax" and "take it easy." That is what many of us did and that is what many of us are *still doing*. The problem with that is, for Black people, the struggle is *never over*.

We are known as the party people of the world, but also known as the people who don't own much. We spend so much time, "having fun", that it's all that is expected of us. People outside of our race have seen us that way for so long that when some of us try to break out of the stereotype, they are puzzled and upset. "Wait. What do you think you're doing? Get back in your box. Who's going to entertain us? You're not funny anymore." "You're being too serious now. And that's just not you!"

If we're ever going to be effective "outside of the box", we're going to have to do it in larger numbers, because that is the only way to be unstoppable. When people put forth a *concerted* effort, it can break down barriers. There is strength in numbers. And we are badly in need of an image change.

Speaking of women's rights gained, it seems like not that long ago, women in America were fighting hard to be recognized as something more that sexual objects. Now that they have won their right to be who they want to be it appears that the only recognition many of them want is to be thought of as "sexy".

The same type of sexual exploitation of women that once came by way of men, is now coming by way of many *women themselves*. Often exploiting *their own* bodies. Even to the point of appearing naked to gain approval and acceptance. As if they're saying, "Look at me. Don't I have a lovely body?" or "Aren't I beautiful?" And while I totally agree that women are beautiful, I wonder what some of these women are thinking.

It's ludicrous to say, "Don't think of these women as sex objects," when they seem to be courting just that type of attention. What I'm really saying is this: Be honest about whatever you're doing. You can't have it both ways. Or can you? We can make laws all over the place, but they are just laws. In order to be safe, we need to be aware of the *laws of nature*.

I have no intention of defending bad behavior by anyone. But if man's sexual attraction to woman wasn't such a strong force, then pornography, strip clubs, and beauty pageants wouldn't be so popular.

The first argument presented by women will be, "I should be able to dress and look as sexy as I want to and not be ogled or threatened by men." In theory and by lawful rights, that is correct. But being theoretically correct does not guarantee your safety. When populations increase, so does the number of different types of people, good and bad, including sexual predators.

In today's society, most of us have learned to criticize things we don't agree with, *in our minds only*. To verbalize it means to make yourself a target of so many groups who will defend anyone's right to do, or say, just about *anything*. There is not much "freedom" in freedom of speech anymore. Only if they like what you're saying.

"Where anything goes; anything grows."

We have developed into a society where the people who should be the most protected are the ones most neglected. By that, I am referring to the women, children, and seniors in America. For many reasons, the family structure is not only being threatened, but *being eroded* at a rapid pace. And it has a lot to do with the neglect of these three very important components that are necessary for a healthy society.

Since women are the ones who carry, birth, and nurture the children, they *should be valued* as the "Mothers of Society." Yet, the climate of male and female relationships of today is seriously in need of repair. And the blame must be shared.

Some men have always treated women terribly. For whatever reasons, some men have been abusive to women as far back as history will take us. What is new, is how women have bought into the abuse by calling themselves, and each other, names like "bitch" and "hoe", while accepting the same treatment from men.

Right away, someone is thinking, "That's only Black women who do that." It's true that these terms used for describing women became acceptable in a bigger way, by the popularity of rap music.

But think again. This was already happening, to some degree before the explosion of rap and has become accepted behavior by *some women of all races. And when you disrespect yourself, it makes it easier for others to disrespect you.* And when they do, you don't have the right to complain because you have forfeited that right by doing it yourself.

As a matter of fact, this practice of women calling themselves these names and allowing others to do the same is so widely accepted that it might seem like knit picking to some people that I even bring it up. That, acceptance, is proof that we are descending, or have descended, into an immoral society. So now the innocent women suffer because of the guilty?

With deep regret I say, "It is a dangerous time in the history of the world, to be a woman." Because of the lack of respect for women, some men believe that they can force themselves on them, anytime they feel like it. And with sex being emphasized, seemingly, everywhere you turn, some men naïvely believe that, "no", *really means*, "yes". The men who still respect women should do their best to protect them from those who don't, or we will all be in trouble.

So many things that women do, appear to be for the purpose of pleasing men. Sometimes their desire to please takes them out of who they *want* to be and makes them portray the role of whom they feel they *need to be,* to please a man. Often being persuaded to do things that they are against, but willing to compromise and do, *to please a man.*

For instance, housewives being so intimidated by strippers that they install dance poles in their homes, trying to keep their men satisfied and out of the clubs. There may be women who do it for other reasons. Only she knows. But I am addressing the ones who do it for the purpose of competing with the strippers.

Because there are so many "willing" women to choose from, these days, it puts the "onus" on men to remain faithful. Which is where it should be. But since the nature of many men is a desire to be with more than one woman, they fail in this department.

And where any part of the family breakdown occurs, the entire family suffers. When the family structure breaks down, it affects more than just the family.

For instance, if a father leaves the family *or is told to leave*, it most often presents a financial burden to be carried by the rest of the extended family members, such as grandparents, or siblings of the mother or father. It was pointed out to me, as a child, that a person can't possibly take care of two households (the man's home and the estranged family's home) on a regular working person's salary.

It is usually the children who suffer the most. If all else fails, welfare often steps in. To the chagrin of the middle and upper class, who are, "Sick of the government using my tax money to take care of these lazy people who sit on their butts all day and do nothing."

The scene in present day America is one where there are so many people vying for your attention in so many areas of life, it's hard to know truth from fiction. There are groups being formed around just about any subject of discussion that you can think of. With so many claiming to have the perfect advice and solutions. "How to raise children", "how to keep your husband," "how to spot cheating", etc. With the biggest problem being, everyone has a different answer.

There was a time when most people were on the same page about these types of things. Now people make claims and have opinions on things that they have no proof of, or nothing concrete to base their opinions on. But that doesn't stop them from being *aggressively opinionated*. Even to the point of being *physically* aggressive. Like harming people who don't feel the same as they do.

The *children* of America, and the world, have become the most vulnerable members of society. I'm speaking of the epidemic of child molestation, child pornography, kidnapping of children, the buying and selling of stolen children. Sometimes not even *stolen* but *sold* by their own parents. Finally, children being murdered.

America is in moral decay. I have heard from some of my detractors that I have a gloomy outlook when it comes to the present state of America. I'm simply painting the picture of the scene that is before me. We can act like it isn't happening, but if so, it will be to the detriment of our children.

There is no question that the children are the future of America, but if we don't do a better job of protecting them from their ever-increasing numbers of predators, we might not be able to recover. At no time in the history of this country, since slavery and lynching, have we faced such a wicked and evil crime, as crimes against children.

We have reached a point where laws are not enough to protect our young ones because the predators are willing to take the risk of getting caught. Maybe because the *laws* are not as strenuous as they should be.

In some cases, the offenders are not even prosecuted, and in cases where they are, they often get lenient sentences. It makes you wonder what is going on with the court systems. Adoption agencies are walking on pins and needles, fretting over peoples' reasons for wanting to adopt, because of the possibility that they could be enabling child molesters.

One of the worst scenarios of all is the possibility of *parents* molesting and abusing their *own* children. And it is happening everyday across America. Like a lot of things going on in our society, we discuss it within our inner circle and move on. Until it happens to one of our own, or someone close to us.

In all honesty, there isn't a lot that we *can do* to prevent it, short of locking our children away in the house. Which isn't practical, considering they must go to school and do things that children are supposed to do. Even that's not safe anymore with schools and playgrounds being predators' favorite hunting spots.

When I hear people say, "You wait. They will get theirs when they get to prison", it bothers me. First because that is hardly true anymore. Sexual offenders in most prisons are in a section with people who have committed sexual offenses also. Secondly because by this time it's already too late for the child. They are often dead or have been traumatized for life. Sometimes going on to perpetrate the same crime on other children as they grow older.

I wish I could think of an answer, but I can't. I also don't believe that a person who commits a child sexual molestation can be rehabilitated. I disagree with the therapists who say they can be. But if a person of credibility says it, then in America, you now have millions who will agree with them.

I believe that a person who thinks that way *ever*, with uncontrollable desires for children, can never control themselves. I hope I'm wrong about it, because it's a horrifying thought if I'm right.

Things are nothing like they were when I was a child of the 50's. Being allowed to *be a child* has everything to do with who I am today. The imagination that I presently have is not a lot different from what it was as a child.

I was *allowed* to dream, unhindered by hardly anything. Even growing up in poverty didn't stop me from dreaming. If anything, it caused me to dream even more.

In the America of today, everybody is so consumed with self and doing their own thing, that they don't have much time to be concerned about anything else. And that is not a statement of rebuke, but one of recognition. Recognizing that life today is such a whirlwind affair that just *trying to keep up*, presents a major challenge.

As far as protecting the children, we need to be aware that the predators are way ahead of most of us, in their planning. Things like becoming scout leaders, elementary school teachers, counselors, pediatricians, youth coaches, principles, and any other profession which places them in the presence of children.

Recognizing this, I have had conversations with my children and grandchildren that were more graphic than I cared to have but felt the necessity to warn them about the dangers beforehand.

I mean no offence to the people in these lines of work who are there to perform a legitimate service, as a matter of fact, I'm thankful for you. But as parents and grandparents, we need to ask questions and do back-ground checks, as much as possible, on people working in close contact with our children.

We, just as importantly, need to have question and answer sessions with our children about their interaction with the adults that they are in contact with. As the saying goes, "An ounce of prevention is worth a pound of cure."

We live in a world where those who are privileged to make the rules are not concerned about much, other than themselves. That leaves the job of protecting ourselves and our loved ones, strictly up to us.

Sometimes it might mean appearing a little eccentric. Asking questions where people don't normally ask questions. But there is no *normal* anymore. We must take the steps to protect our loved ones. Even at the risk of appearing different from the norm.

I can't tell you when it happened but it's obvious that America no longer holds our senior citizens in high regards, the way we used to. If you want proof, just look at the increase in the numbers of nursing homes and senior citizen assisted living facilities. They are suddenly big business.

I can remember when putting an elderly family member in a nursing home was something that people would only do, when they couldn't possibly care for them anymore. And it carried a certain amount of shame with it. Because you knew people would say you're "dumping them off" on somebody else. I remember statements like, "My mother will *never* go to a nursing home."

At a time when people are said to be living longer, why do we have so many seniors needing to be in these facilities? The answer, like everything else, is money. One of the main reasons is, in most households, it is required that both spouses work, in situations where there *are* two people, in order to maintain their lifestyle. Leaving no one at home to care for a senior family member.

What I fail to understand is how did we lose *respect* for the seniors, the way we have? There was a time when senior family members were held in high regards. In fact, they were the most respected ones *in the family*. No one cussed around them. They were asked questions about how they did certain things and any advice was well-taken and appreciated.

Now they are treated, for the most part, like they don't know *anything*. Often getting more respect from their grandchildren than their grown children that they raised. I remember when council from the elderly was considered valuable. *To me it still is.*

Let's talk about patriotism. Ahh patriotism. You know. Standing and saluting the flag at almost any and every civic gathering, including schools. Oh, I've *heard* that *some* schools have brought it back. Wait a minute. "Brought it back?" Where was it? The sad truth is The Pledge of Allegiance, as it is called, when we salute and say our allegiance to the American flag, has been banned in many schools throughout America.

Why? I'm not clear on that one. But I remember when everyone in class had to stand and pledge allegiance to the flag of the United States of America. Hey. Even that sounds strange. When was the last time that you heard, "The *United* States of America?" Mostly, these days, if you hear anything other than America, it's "The States."

We are so short in the nationalism department that people who are naturalized American citizens are openly displaying and honoring the flags of the countries from which they came. Alone, or *along with* the American flag.

Not to mention the large numbers of confederate flags, flying throughout These "*United*" States of America. Once again, I take no joy in this. I consider it a wakeup call to the people who actually *care* about holding our Union together. But just like any other complaint or critique made about America, by an African American, in some circles it will be felt that I have no right to speak on that.

And that, itself, is a big part of the problem. The fact that we, as an ethnically divided country, are placing the emphasis on too many of the wrong things which *keep us divided* and unable to deal with our *real* problems, realistically.

I know this is going to sound corny, but what if we woke up and all of the memories of our past racial rivalries, hatred, and animosity were gone. Completely gone. What would we do? Probably be so relieved and unburdened that we would find ourselves walking around with the most stupid grins on our faces. Far from the snarls and frowns that many people wear today, like masks. We would look at each other and know that, "Oh you had that epiphany too!?" But life is real, and we'll probably have to find another way to *that* place. But find it we must, or we're not going to last.

"We're all in this together. Like it or not."

CHAPTER 7

American: Not Also American

Black soldiers returned home to America from World War II, feeling triumphant because of the role they played in helping to defeat our country's enemies. African Americans fought bravely and helped in many ways to win the war, expecting that this would improve their status back home. But it was not so.

There was yet another war to be fought. This one *at home* and a different *type* of war. The war against Jim Crow. Institutionalized racism in this country. While some are pleased to say that it existed only in the southern U.S., the reality is that it was practiced, in one way or another, all over the country. Whatever the case, it had a unifying effect on the Black community.

The general thinking among Black people was that, "If we don't do it for ourselves, no one else is going to do it for us." They began to adopt another way of fighting, by taking a more focused approach toward educating their children.

If the cycle of ignorance and poverty were ever going to be broken, then education was the way to accomplish that goal. Also, since so many of the Black parents had been born in the southern states, they seldom had the privilege to attend school, themselves. Working instead, on plantations and farms to help the family to survive poverty. Because of not having had the opportunity, *they insisted* that their children, not only *attend* school, but apply themselves to every bit of learning that was offered.

The schools were segregated between Blacks and Whites and the plan was to educate the so-called Negro, to make them fit in better, but not prosper as much as Whites. Just enough to keep them from dragging the country down with their ignorance, but not enough to make them feel empowered or "uppity."

This segregation sat well with Black people, when it came to schooling. Giving their educators the time, and environment, to work closely with their own. Molding and shaping the minds of the Black youth. More often, than not, the teachers had full permission from the parents, to use whatever they deemed necessary to achieve success with the students. Even corporal punishment.

Liberal minded White people felt good about themselves because they were helping the Negro to rise above their history of slavery in America. On the other hand, the adversaries to this type of thinking felt that the Negro was having it *too* good. "Hell, before you know it, they'll think they're as good as *us*." Allowing Black people to compete on *an equal basis* wasn't appealing. Not even, to many of the "liberal minded" Whites.

In every society, there is competition for placement in jobs, political positions, institutions of higher learning and many other things that people of that society need to work at, in order to make a living. It has been proven that the membership of the Ku Klux Klan is at its highest when the economy is not faring well, and jobs are hard to find. This is because Whites on the lower economic level, are being made to feel that "*their*" jobs are being taken by Blacks and immigrants.

This type of thinking was fueled by the sentiment which made it possible for the lynch mob mentality to flourish. It is much easier to bring people together, if there is a common cause, even to do something as cruel as lynching another human being. That common cause was White people feeling that Black people were depriving them of their opportunity to work and provide for themselves or were about to do that.

Also, the thought of living close to Black People was not appealing to most of the White American population. Some examples of their reasons were: "They bring down the standard of living." "They don't *want* to work." "The Blacks just want to rape our women." "They're too *dumb* to educate."

Even though slavery had been abolished, by law, there were still other laws which had been put on the books to keep the "Negro" in his or her place. More so, in "his" place, than in "her" place. I say this because, even back then, the Black woman was free to do more things and go more places than her male counterpart.

Slander can be a very effective tactic to use when trying to prevent people from coming together. Some of the controversies that exist between Black men and women even today, were introduced when slavery was in its heyday.

Because some Black woman were spending a lot of time in the slave owner's house and raising his children, cleaning the house, and being told that her husband was a "no count" shiftless lazy son of a gun, she sometimes felt superior to him. But some of them just kept quiet and only *pretended* to agree with the slave owner.

After enslaving and bringing people from the African continent to do their manual labor, America, as an industrial nation, began to prosper tremendously. But the prosperity was one-sided. Because of slaves having no legal rights to anything, all of the Africans' inventions or ideas, which researching of *true history* has proven to be many, were credited to the slave owners or other White people.

In an effort, to better *control* "their Negroes", the Europeans forced them to give up any semblance of their former culture, even, and especially, their languages. They were forbidden to learn to read and write English, in order to keep them as ignorant as possible, about what was going on around them.

Education of any kind was forbidden to the slaves and even *after* slavery, it was conveyed to educators that the so-called Negro was not easily educated and if they must be, bring them along slowly. The reality was that it was never intended for the African Americans to get on equal footing with their White counterparts, so since education was the best way to achieve that equal footing, it was being denied in subtle, but effective, ways.

Some White colleges and universities were founded with money gained from the benefits of slave labor, and for obvious reasons those same institutions were not exactly welcoming to former slaves or their offspring. That resistance, though vehemently denied, still exists to this day in subtle but still effective ways. Things like, "Where is your student I.D.?", "Are you sure you're a student here?" "I've never seen you on campus before."

The following is an excerpt from, "Shackled legacy: Universities and The Slave Trade" a story written by Stephen Smith & Kate Ellis
https://www.apmreports.org/story/2017/09/04/shackled-legacy

Dozens of American colleges and universities are investigating their historic ties to the slave trade and debating how to atone.

Profits from slavery and related industries helped fund some of the most prestigious schools in the Northeast, including Harvard, Columbia, Princeton and Yale. And in many southern states — including the University of Virginia — enslaved people built college campuses and served faculty and students.

- End of article

As a testament to their intention for the former slaves to achieve higher learning, Black churches partnered with an abolitionist organization called the America Missionary Association and the Freedmen's Bureau, an agency of the United States Department of War, in 1865 to establish the first "Negro" college in this country. This was in order to allow the Africans to be educated amongst themselves and become less of a burden to the American system by being educated.

- The following excerpt is taken from the National Museum of African America History & Culture at the Smithsonian Institute: https://nmaahc.si.edu/blog/five-things-know-hbcu-edition#targetText=History,Association%20and%20the%20Freedmen's%20Bureau.&targetText=Shaw%20University%E2%80%93%E2%80%93founded%20in%20Raleigh,organized%20after%20the%20 Civil%20War.

Historically black colleges and universities—commonly called "HBCUs"—are defined by the **Higher Education Act of 1965** as, *"...any historically black or university that was established prior to 1964, whose principal mission was, and is, the education of black Americans, and that is accredited by a nationally recognized accrediting agency or association determined by the Secretary [of Education]..."*

History

1. The first colleges for African Americans were established largely through the efforts of black churches with the support of the **American Missionary Association** and the **Freedmen's Bureau**. The second **Morrill Act of 1890** required states—especially former confederate states—to provide land-grants for institutions for black students if admission was not allowed elsewhere. As a result, many Historically Black Colleges and Universities (HBCUs) were founded.

2. Between 1861 and 1900 more than 90 institutions of higher learning were established. Shaw University—founded in Raleigh, North Carolina, in 1865—was the first black college organized after the Civil War. Other schools include: **Talladega College**, **Howard University**, **Morehouse College** and **Hampton University.**

- END OF ARTICLE

Historically Black Colleges *became*, and *still remain,* cornerstones of pride that Black people point to when feeling the need to show that even though we ascended *from* slavery, this is part of whom we have *become*. Sadly, it is not the case for the majority of Black people in America. It's not really the case for most of the mass population, at large, of any race.

Therein lies the major source of most of our problems in this country. *Ignorance.* A mostly uneducated populous. Lack of education causes individuals to make uninformed choices. This can be, and is proving to be, a very serious problem. If you don't *have* an opinion of your own, someone is standing by to *give* you one.

When the opportunity to receive even a grade school or high school education presented itself, Black parents tried to make sure their children got as much learning as was available. The Civil rights act kicked in and it appeared that nothing could stop us.

Then came the onslaught of many carefully devised plans to penetrate the nucleus of collective African American intelligence and prosperity. As individuals, we are not a threat to the system. As a unified group, we have the potential to achieve much more.

But after seeing the successes of Dr. Martin Luther King, Malcolm X, and the Black Panther Party, plans were put in place to make sure that type of collective Black strength and togetherness was never to take root again.

Dismissing and labeling the Black Panther Party as racists and a threat to the White citizenry of America gave the government the excuse that they needed to destroy them. Nationwide. But it was all based on lies.

The Black Panther Party was not established to do anything but stand for the rights of Black people across America. Many of them were college educated, with the intent of erasing illiteracy and poverty in the Black slums of America. I don't expect people who don't already know that, to believe it. Mainly, because of the smear campaign put out by our government. But if you are willing to do the proper research, you will find it to be the truth.

Having already established reading programs and breakfast programs so that hungry children could eat before attending school in the morning. For that they were labeled as trying to indoctrinate them into their ideology. Which was labeled as socialism, a word that is used to scare people away from you by equating you with desiring to be communist. Many lives have been destroyed in America by the application of those two words. Without even a trace of truth.

As proof of what they stood for, I challenge anyone to research and find any *real* evidence to show that the Black Panther Party ever tried to violently overthrow the American government. Some will say, "That's because they were shut down so efficiently by the police and FBI." If you believe that, you don't know Black people. If that had been their intent, they wouldn't have publicly displayed their weapons and would have mounted *covert* attacks on the authorities.

The Black Panthers' display of weapons was to show that they understood the *Constitution*. "The right to bear arms." Instead, the government *mounted the attacks on them*. Killing innocent people in the process. Which is nothing new. The history exists if you care to look in the right places. *They hid it in books.*

The pre-dawn raid by, Chicago police, which took the lives of Chairman Fred Hampton and Mark Clark, comes to mind. Resulting in a seven-figure settlement payout to their families. I think that alone is proof enough that the government murdered them. And still they contested the verdict in a case that lasted for so many years that the families of Fred Hampton and Mark Clark wound up exhausting the settlement in legal fees.

The Following is an excerpt that gives some insight into how the FBI felt about Chairman Fred Hampton.

Ward Churchill; Jim Vander Wall (1988). Agents of Repression: The FBI's Secret Wars Against the Black Panther Party and the American Indian Movement. p. 66. ISBN 0-89608-293-8.

While Hampton impressed many of the people with whom he came into contact as an effective leader and talented communicator, those very qualities marked him as a major threat in the eyes of the FBI Hence, the bureau began keeping close tabs on his activities. Subsequent investigations have shown that FBI chief J. Edgar Hoover was determined to prevent formation of a cohesive Black movement in the United States. Hoover saw the Panthers, Young Patriots, Young Lords, and similar radical coalitions forged by Hampton in Chicago as a frightening steppingstone toward the creation of such a revolutionary body that could, in its strength, cause a radical change in the U.S. government.

The FBI opened a file on Hampton in 1967. Hampton's mother's phone was tapped in February 1968, and Hampton was placed on the Bureau's "<u>Agitator Index</u>" a "key militant leader" by May.

- **End of Article**

The line that draws most of my attention is:

"Hoover saw the Panthers, Young Patriots, Young Lords, and similar radical coalitions forged by Hampton in Chicago as a frightening steppingstone toward the creation of such a revolutionary body that could, in its strength, cause a radical change in the U.S. government." **The U.S. Government could *use* a radical change. In a more all-inclusive direction.**

Malcolm was assassinated because he wielded so much power, control, and influence, that they felt him capable of mounting such an attack. Once again, they painted a picture of a racist madman just waiting for the chance to destroy White America. When in fact he died seeking truth and for taking a real stand *against* racism. But America, as an institution, hates the truth and covers it up and denies it, except when it serves her purpose. And racism? Well that's at the core of her existence.

Which brings us to Martin. Since Dr. King campaigned for non-violence he couldn't be publicly labeled as an *enemy* of the state, *although he was*. They hated him for what he stood for. Which was non-violence. "Come on. Just give us one good reason to blow your head off." But he didn't. Secondly, they hated him for what he was asking for. Freedom. And he had the nerve to do it in an intellectually, eloquent manner. Martin used words that most people didn't even know existed. And because non-violence is hard to speak against, they had to be satisfied with calling him a "troublemaker", for getting the people stirred up.

So, Dr. King had to be assassinated by a "lone gunman". That way, everyone, including the ones who wanted him dead and very well may have ordered his death, could act hurt and surprised. "Who would kill such a good man," "Poor peace-loving Martin." Cut the crap. You hated him and you know it! Every time we put our hopes in a deliverer, a "Moses", so to speak. You kill them. *No matter what race.* John and Robert Kennedy are prime examples.

It seems that with every assassination of leaders sympathetic to the Black cause, another part of our hope is diminished. In the process, many have lost faith in the system. So much so, that Americans, of all races, don't really aspire to much that is descent now days. Their attitude seems to be, "Let me enjoy the moment. Who knows what tomorrow will bring?"

Only a select few show any interest in getting educated these days, and even then, tend to be inspired only by how much money they can make. Money seems to be the motivation for *most people* of today's America.

Some years back, during a conversation, with a close friend of mine, Norman Richmond, who is also African American, he let out a bombshell, "Hey Man, if you wanted to hide something from a Black person, where would you put it?" "Where?" I replied. "In a book!" was his answer. I became upset by that. Which was the exact response that he was looking for! "Made you mad didn't it?" Yes. It did, for a couple of reasons. Number one I, personally *love* reading. In the second place, I was upset, because in so many ways, it was true. I began to wonder, when, and how it *became* true.

As a Black child, of the 50's, because we were less than one hundred years removed from slavery, and, because of the newly granted opportunity to achieve an education, we were persuaded, by our parents, or guardians, to work as hard as we could at our studies. They were convinced, that education is the way out of destitution and, one way, or another, you were going to get plenty of it, *whether you wanted to, or not*.

When it came to schooling, we were treated as if the teachers were an extension of our family. Like parents away from home. They had the authority, from our parents, *and the school board*, to make us learn, by any means necessary, even by physical punishment.

And they did their jobs very well. By the time I finished the fifth grade, I had the basic reading and mathematical skills required to begin higher learning. I have since learned, by talking to some of my friends, that some White students were subjected to the same type of strict discipline as the Black students were.

Not only were we taught our curriculum, but also manners and behavioral skills. Girls were taught to be ladies and boys were taught to be gentlemen. Our only choice in the matter was to do as we were told. Personal hygiene was taught along with health issues.

We didn't have video games or calculators. Watching television, largely cartoons, was our most popular mode of entertainment, along with reading. This is not to say there's anything wrong with *some* video games and calculators. The main problem is that playing video games has replaced studying, for a lot of children *and* is taking up a lot of time in the lives of many young adults. Calculators have replaced the worthwhile challenge of learning times tables and basic mathematics.

As it is well-documented, the times of my childhood were filled with much struggle for African Americans, trying to achieve our civil rights and still being thought of by many, as being only slightly removed from slavery.

The desegregation of schools was a very big issue, and one that seemed to be a great way to right some wrongs. The main objective was to give African American students access to better facilities, such as better books and better learning environments. And have them interact with White children and vice versa.

At first it threatened to tear the country apart. A lot of White parents, and White people in general, resisted to the point of violence. The first Black children to attend all-White schools had to have guards escort them to school. Mostly the National Guard, because they were military and could be trusted to do their job. The Black students were called names, spat on, and in some instances physically attacked.

Eventually, realizing that they couldn't prevent school integration, the active protests were abandoned. Replaced by more subtle attempts at preventing integration. Sometimes refusing to send White children to formerly all-Black schools. Rezoning school districts. Moving to their own private enclaves. Then, after a while, integration seemed to be working.

As the years went by, the newfound freedom of the African American students, in general, began to work against them. No longer were they subjected to the nurturing and the admonition of the African American teachers, who felt the need to *force* them to perform up to the standards they had set for them. They were now allowed to not even *attend* school, in many cases, if they didn't want to.

The laws had changed, as far as the authority that the teachers had over the students. Laws were put in place that said any physical contact with a student, by a teacher, could be deemed, child abuse. Those same laws were applied to parenting. Plus, only a Black teacher was going to get away with certain types of disciplining of a Black student anyway. Otherwise, it could be thought of as racism.

By this time, the Black teachers' attitudes had changed to the point of, "We can't get away with that type of discipline anymore, because people are watching." Some of the students became incorrigible, to the point of, "I don't have to listen, and you can't make me!" Also, somewhere along the way, the services of truant officers were appearing to no longer be required.

I imagine some of you are even wondering, "What *is* a truant officer?" A truant officer was a person deputized, by law, to make sure all students, of school age, attended school, on a regular basis. If the students didn't attend school on an acceptable basis, the students *and* the parents were subjected to punishment by law. Juvenile detention for the student, for non-attendance, and monetary fines, and possibly jail time for parents, who didn't adhere to the laws.

Needless to say, when the *laws* regarding attending school became lax, so did the attendance. An uneducated society is a dysfunctional society. And so, began the downward spiral of the Black community. *Education*, in the Black community, was the main catalyst, as I previously pointed out, for reaching towards hope. With a decent education, a person could enjoy a higher standard of living, through having a better type of job. There is hope for breaking the welfare cycle, in the poorest communities. Once again, through education.

An uneducated society is ripe for the invasion of stimulants, which provide a false sense of escape from one's reality. These stimulants came into the Black community, by way of, drugs, alcohol, and illicit sex. And they have brought all kinds of destruction with them.

I believe that the liquor stores came in before the drugs, because of the ease with which a liquor license could be obtained, in the Black community. Then came the drugs, in many forms, marijuana, cocaine, and heroin, were the most popular drugs of the time. Since then, there are even more of them. So constantly being added to the list that they're too numerous to keep up with.

Some of the leaders, of the Black community began to say that the drugs and alcohol, which were becoming easier to get, were not there by coincidence, but by design, from outside of the community. Placed there, to *destroy* the community. The fact is, there are even some government documents, which have been uncovered, supporting that theory.

It appears that the Black community has not only, been allowed to, but has been encouraged and been assisted in spiraling out of control. And the motive appears to be twofold. For profit and keeping Black people from becoming competition on an intellectual level by trying to purposely keep them uneducated. "Who cares if you don't go to school or get a job? If you want to be poor and destitute, go ahead and *be* a failure. You're not hurting me."

I beg to differ. It's not only hurting you. It's hurting you, me, and every citizen of this country. By making us weaker in every sense. *Physically weaker*, because of so many sicknesses associated with drug use. Clinics have been established strictly for the sake of treating drug addiction, so that lets us know just how serious the problem is. Ultimately our tax dollars are paying for the treatment. *Weaker mentally* because of the toll which drug abuse has taken on your mind, and just plain lack of interest in anything, except what you are addicted to.

Think about the American resilience and cohesion which I spoke of that was believed to have saved us during WWII. You would be hard pressed to get even a handful of people to agree on *almost anything*, these days. There is more *division* going on in this country than *togetherness*. We're so confused that some of our own citizens are going abroad to be trained to fight against us.

We need not only *ask* why but give the question some real thought. It's easy to write them off as 'unpatriotic hot heads', but I prefer to know what left them so disenfranchised that they would even consider it? One of the simple answers is, they feel left out of the decision-making process of our government. Be it real, or perceived.

If you take away the things that create a feeling of patriotism in a country, it no longer *feels like a country*. Just a bunch of people going in different directions, with nothing holding them together.

As a child in school we said the Pledge of Allegiance, every morning. Along with singing the Star- Spangled Banner. It is no longer required, *and in some cases, students are not allowed, to do either.* There is not much holding us together anymore. Most peoples' loyalty now days is only to family and friends. And that, in a very small circle.

When a democratic country like America, invites and accepts people from all parts of the world, it needs to have a strong sense of nationalism, in order not to lose its own identity. Different nationalities bring with them, different customs and laws that they conform to.

This can be very divisive in a country with a weak doctrine, which America has become, but is *unwilling to accept the fact.* A lack of patriotism is blamed on everything and everybody else, when it's mainly the fault of our American leadership for not continuing to teach patriotism to the young.

The only Americans speaking of nationalism now days are the White supremist groups advocating for "White pride" and for keeping America White. It seems our "leaders" have forgotten about nationalism altogether.

If I'm painting a dismal picture, it's not because I'm happy about it. I do know of people who are waiting for the "fall of America", but I'm not one of them. It hurts to see where this country is heading. The "chickens coming home to roost" syndrome might be true, but I don't get any joy from it. I'm a born African American. With just as much emphasis on the American, as the African aspect of my heritage. I'm a Black man who because of my history, and birthright, in this America, has earned the right to be here. It was purchased with the blood, sweat and tears of my ancestors. *That is my passport and birth certificate!*

But, I emphasize, *my* peoples' involvement was not voluntary, and the struggle *was beyond* intense. There are huge differences between the Africans' role and the Europeans' role in building this country into the America which it has become. Never-the-less the participation is undeniable from both parties. And since the Natives of these two continents were here before *any of the rest of us*, their claim for the right to be here speaks for itself.

Some people work more closely together when facing danger from without. When they have a common threat. But when the danger has passed, they drift apart. Such seems to be the case with Black people and America in general.

After slavery, there were plenty of reasons for the Black race to work together in whatever ways they could. After all, very few people, other than their own, had a reason *or desire* to help them. At first, they were a peculiarity, walking about, looking, and feeling lost. *Always* in the way, as far as White people were concerned. Add to that, the threat of being attacked, or killed, at the hands of a White lynch mob.

When Black America and White America are not at war with another country, and fighting jointly, they are fighting against each other. There are Black people in America who feel that, because of slavery, and the racism directed at Black people by some White people, it's not racist to hate White people. *Hating a people, as a race, is racism*, and racism, by its very definition is wrong, and never right, no matter where or whom it comes from. And for whatever reason.

As a country, America has built up a false sense of security and acceptance for its citizens. When it *really* only applies to *White America*. And even many of *the poor* of *White America*'s sense of belonging is questioned.

With the history of America, from as far back as its inception, it appears that the ones who shape the future of the country are more interested in *segregation* than even *education*. More concerned with making and keeping it a *White* and racially divided country, than a strong and unified one. And to call it ignorance would be denying the truth, because it is calculated, intentioned, and *institutionalized* bigotry.

In some ways though, we African Americans have contributed to our own slow pace of progress. Which is not saying, by any means, that we have not had to deal with many stumbling blocks *placed* in front of us. In all fairness, there have always been those African Americans who were about the business of taking advantage of whatever glimmer of opportunity was before them, sometimes *creating* an opportunity where there was none.

Which brings to mind, a young man by the name of Tyler Perry. My awareness of him came by way of his "Madea" movies. To be totally honest, my first impression of him was, "After how Black people have been stereotyped and exploited, in the name of comedy, by White movie makers, how can a Black man do the same thing to us?"

Then, I realized that there was much more truth and realism to what Mr. Perry was doing, than anything else I had seen in the past. But the part that I am most impressed about, is how he has invested the money that he generated from his success. Not only did he have the concept, he also has the vision.

Mr. Tyler Perry has become the most successful single movie maker of recent years. His studio properties located in Atlanta, Georgia, sit on an area that is bigger than the three largest in Hollywood combined. Which makes it the largest in the country. I have recently learned that one of the Democratic debates for the 2020 presidential election was held there. No matter what anyone thinks of his journey, he has become so successful that the *end positively justifies the means*.

The other side of the coin is the Black people who have felt the best way to deal with the oppression is to treat life like "One big party." The trouble with parties is you must know where they should end, and real life begins. And each individual needs to know when to call their own "timeout." We have taught the world how to party, all the while being left out of the party that matters most. The party of *realistically* enjoying life, with *all* the trappings. Like houses, substantial bank accounts, being able to travel the world, and this might seem surprising to say, having a decent life insurance policy.

If you were to ask the average poor Black person why they haven't achieved more, the answer will often be that it's because someone held them back. Usually, "The White man".
And believe me, as a Black person, I can attest to a certain amount of truth in that. But where *that* truth *ends*, another one *begins*. The second truth is; *self-help*, which is most important and can only be denied *to you, by you*. Which means, if you are not doing something to *help* yourself, then *you* are the main one *depriving yourself*.

   I firmly believe that I have a certain amount of power over my own destiny, according to what I choose to do with my time. And one most important thing that I must do is, either *remove* things that block my path or figure out a way around them. And since there is always some work involved, I must be prepared to rise to the occasion.

   One thing necessary for building any type of intellectual foundation is reading. Knowing *how* to read is a good start but it won't get you there. It is not enough to *know how* to read. *Application* is the saving grace of reading. If you *can* read, you need to *use* your reading skills, allowing them to serve you well. Reading quality materials, mixed with a heavy dose of common sense, can do wonders for your upward progression in life.

For some reason, progress in one area, seems to bring neglect in another area. When it became necessary for both parents to maintain jobs and no adult supervision was taking place at home, the affects were felt in declining grades, poor attendance, and in many other negative ways. Women fought very hard to gain an equal place in society that would give them the freedom to pursue their own careers and agendas the same as men had the right to do. And they won their freedom. Along with women's freedom came *children's freedom*.

What do I mean? When women's work drew them outside of the home, children were left on their own. Some didn't fare so well. This is not to say, "A woman's place is in the house". I wouldn't be so naïve. But I say it to say progress can be costly. And sometimes the price can break you. Society has benefited greatly from having women being free to choose whatever careers they want. Some, while doing double duty as working women *and mothers*, and handling both very well.

Some women have children, some don't, and some women want to, but can't. Some *choose* not to. But there is one thing that is undeniable when it comes to children. Most require nurturing in order to feel complete. And although my personal belief is that *women* are better nurturers, a man whose heart is in the right place, can put forth a pretty convincing case.

Along with this new "freedom" for the children came a penchant for testing boundaries. And just like that, a term called "juvenile delinquency" began being tossed about. It was a new way of describing children who got into trouble. Usually, breaking laws. As soon as Hollywood got in on the act and made some movies like, "Rebel Without A Cause", starring James Dean, juvenile delinquency suddenly looked glamorous and the thing to be. Playing "hooky" (not attending, but pretending to go to school), something most students would have been too afraid to do in the past, was now one of the things that made a student look "cool" in the eyes of some others.

Teenagers started smoking and drinking, illegally, of course, trying to act and look more adult. Imitating what they saw grownups do. So much for education. When something is required, but not desired, it feels like you are being forced to do it against your will. Such was the case of trying to educate rebellious children who felt that they were being held back from adulthood, to which in their minds, they felt like they had already arrived. Then there was the peer pressure. "You're not allowed to do *anything*! My parents will let me do whatever I want! Actually, they can't stop me."

So much of this type of discussion with someone who is respected as being "in the know", can poison the mind of a student on the edge of trying to decide whether they want to pursue an education or not. To young impressionable minds, visuals can be very persuasive too. Even with adults, if you put it (whatever it is) in a nice enough package, you're more likely to make a sale. This notion wasn't lost on the cigarette and alcohol companies, who began to glamourize their products through packaging and by way of "slick" commercials.

I remember when I was a student in elementary school, having a pretty teacher leaning over my shoulder to explain things and her breath smelling like cigarettes. Believe it or not, being reeled in first, by her looks, and not knowing the real danger of smoking, I thought that was what a *"real woman's"* breath was supposed to smell like. So, there you have it. The "nice package" was the selling point.

Observing life's lessons, I've concluded that people who have families or spouses and achieve success, through hard work, are usually not the greatest of husbands, fathers, wives, or mothers. It's very difficult to be. To become *successful* at *anything* takes up so much of a person's time that they are more likely to be spread thin in other areas of their life.

Especially their personal life. It's like driving and texting at the same time and trying to do both well. It's not *possible* to do both at the same time and do a good job. Both require your *undivided attention* and your attention *must be divided* between them to even attempt both.

Of course, there is no excuse for being in the home and having *time* for interacting with your family and still not making use of that time. I sincerely admire people who can mentor their own family and still have some attention left for other young people, who may not have parents, or whose parents might fall under the, "don't have time" banner. As long as it gets done and leaves someone feeling better about themselves and motivated, everyone is a winner.

There is a word that is often over-used, in America, and that word is, "customary." With so many things having been put in place for all the wrong reasons, being "customary" is holding this country back in a great way. If what is customary isn't beneficial to all, it needs to be changed. The only thing that should be the same is the pursuit of patriotism and dedication to oneness, as citizens who love the same country.

Yet patriotism is often thought of in terms of race or ethnicity. "They're taking away *our* country." The reason it feels that way is because, while you were so tightly holding onto racism and considering it to be patriotism, *true* patriotism got neglected and lost.

Now you're fighting, and stockpiling for, *a war that only exists in your mind*. It sure would be nice to feel included in this country called America. To be able to breathe without being accused of taking someone else's air. In the words of a great man, Dr. Martin Luther King Jr., "We must learn to live together as brothers or perish together as fools."

"Style is everything"

CHAPTER 8

Pop Culture

America has always had the need for something to ease the tension. Which has *always been with us*. Entertainment has been one of things that can make us forget, *temporarily*. One of the earliest forms of entertainment was gathering around to listen to someone sing, dance, or play an instrument. Often a banjo or guitar. The dance might be an Irish or Scottish jig, if the dancers were White. An African tribal dance if the performers were Black. The singing could be religious songs, storytelling folk songs, or songs remembered from England. Songs from Africa were not allowed. As a way of suppressing the African culture while preventing the slaves from, "secret communication".

Is it possible that this need to laugh and feel good about ourselves is part of the reason for our rich American entertainment heritage of today? I think so. Diamonds are forged out of intense heat and there is no denying that America's unfolding history has been filled with violence and tension.

Still, whether it be movies, music, or sports, America has been at the forefront of many forms of entertainment for a very long time. Yet, there's no getting around the fact that the same thing which makes us so rich in culture is the source of much of our misery. Our racial and ethnic diversity.

The thing that has made us strong for so long (ethnic diversity) is beginning to weaken us, because of the inability of American leadership to *accept that diversity*. So much so that our enemies are prepared and waiting to take advantage of that same divisive spirit that dwells among us.

A foreign power (Russia) was proven to have interfered with our most recent presidential election by exploiting our *own* divisiveness. In this instance it was our political differences that were used against us. While the ensuing debate about that occurrence has caused even more division, the real question should be, "What if they decide to exploit our weakest point? America's Achilles heel. Our racial division." Which they probably have plans to do.

Because of that same ethnic diversity and having so much knowledge and talent to draw from, America has been first in many innovations and inventions that have influenced the rest of the world.

Made up of people from *all parts* of the world, America has been fortunate in reaping the benefits from the different cultural aspects that have been brought by the people. In this chapter we will show how America's diversity in ethnicity is her strength, more so than her weakness.

One of our earliest forms of sophisticated entertainment was theater. With its roots in Greece, The Roman Empire, and England, it became, and remains, one of America's fascinations. Getting its start in the larger cities across the country, especially New York.

The use of theater, like many other forms of entertainment wasn't *always* sophisticated. For a while there was a seedier, even bawdy element of theater, producing what could hardly be called "plays", because of their content. Which didn't require much "acting" in the conventional sense of the word. Women appeared on stage partially dressed. The dialogue, if any, consisted of crude sexual "jokes" and inuendo. The performances were limited to mostly metropolitan areas where they were considered to be lewd and offensive to many "decent" folks.

They were frequented, mostly by men, because of the sexual innuendo and what would have been at that time, considered to be, "loose women." More than anything else, they were legal sex shows. And sometimes crossing the line, they became *illegal* and were shut down, usually until a fine was paid.

Some of the Hollywood movie stars got their start in "burlesque", as this type of theater was called. Mae West comes to mind as the most famous one. Bringing the same, not so subtle, sexually themed jokes to the *big* screen. Lines like, "Is that a gun in your pocket or are you just happy to see me?"

As the popularity of burlesque grew, there were shows that went on tour and did very well, box office-wise. The following article sheds some light on how burlesque got its start in America.

Sources for the following article: Hoffos, Signe and Moulder, Bob. "Desperately Seeking Lydia" and "Appreciating Lydia", Archived 2011-05-13 at the Wayback Machine *The Friends of Kensal Green Cemetery Magazine*, Vol. 43, Autumn 2006, pp. 1–7

"Burlesque show", *Encyclopædia Britannica*, Online Library Edition, accessed 16 February 2011subscription required

American burlesque shows were originally an offshoot of Victorian burlesque. The English genre had been successfully staged in New York from the 1840s, and it was popularised by a visiting British burlesque troupe, <u>Lydia Thompson</u> and the "Blondes", beginning in 1868.[32] New York burlesque shows soon incorporated elements and the structure of the popular <u>minstrel shows</u>. They consisted of parts: first, songs and ribald comic sketches by low comedians; second, assorted <u>olios</u> and male acts, such as acrobats, magicians and solo singers; and third, chorus numbers and sometimes a burlesque in the English style on politics or a current play. The entertainment was usually concluded by an exotic dancer or a wrestling or boxing match.[33]

While burlesque went out of fashion in England towards the end of the 19th century, to be replaced by <u>Edwardian musical comedy</u>, the style of burlesque flourished, but with increasing focus on female nudity. Exotic "cooch" dances were brought in, ostensibly Syrian in origin. The entertainments were given in clubs and cabarets, as well as music halls and theatres. By the early 20th century, there were two national circuits of burlesque shows competing with the v<u>audeville</u> circuit, as well as resident companies New York, such as <u>Minsky's</u> at the Winter Garden.[33]

- **End of Article**

An excerpt from: **Herbert Ashbury,** *The Gangs of New York* **(New York: Knopf, 1929).**In the United States and elsewhere, the can-can achieved popularity in music halls, where it was danced by groups of women in choreographed routines. This style was imported back into France in the 1920s for the benefit of tourists, and the "French Cancan" was born—a highly choreographed routine lasting ten minutes or more, with the opportunity for individuals to display their "specialities". The main moves are the high kick or battement, the *rond de jambe* (quick rotary movement of lower leg with knee raised and skirt held up), the *port d'armes* (turning on one leg, while grasping the other leg by the ankle and holding it almost vertically), the cartwheel and the grand écart (the flying or jump splits). It has become common practice for dancers to scream and yelp while performing the can-can.

The can-can was introduced in America on 23 December 1867 by Giuseppina Morlacchi, dancing as a part of *The Devil's Auction* at the Theatre Comique in Boston. It was billed as "Grand Gallop Can-Can, composed and danced by Mlles. Morlacchi, Blasina, Diani, Ricci, Baretta ... accompanied with cymbals and triangles by the coryphees and corps de ballet." The new dance received an enthusiastic reception.

By the 1890s the can-can was out of style in New York dance halls, having been replaced by the hoochie coochie.[43]

- **End of Article**

Preceding, *and during*, this period came minstrel shows and vaudeville, which were very cruel in their portrayals of Black people. A Jewish minstrel/actor by the name of Al Jolson even performed songs like "Mammy" while wearing blackface paint, with huge white lips. And evidently some people must have thought of it as acceptable entertainment. At the top of his career he was referred to as the "world's greatest entertainer." Really?! It is said that although his audiences were receptive to the style of music he was performing, they didn't want to see or hear it performed by the originators. Black people. And when Black actors appeared on stage, they too, were forced to wear blackface because the White audiences *demanded that they wear it.*

Contributors to the following article: Moss, Robert F. (20 October 2000). "Was Al Jolson 'Bamboozled'?". *Los Angeles Times*. Retrieved 22 September 2018.

Rogin, Michael (Spring 1992). "Blackface, White Noise: The Jewish Jazz Singer Finds His Voice". *Critical Inquiry*. University of Chicago Press. 18 (3): 417–453. doi:10.1086/448640. JSTOR 1343811.

The History of Minstrelsy : Al Jolson · USF Library Special & Digital Collections Exhibits".

Wesley, Charles H. (March 1960). "Background and achievement for Negro-Americans". The Crisis. 67 (3): 137. These concepts 'fixed a stage tradition of the Negro as irresponsible, loud-laughing, shuffling banjo playing, singing, dancing sort of a being.' These impressions were continued through the antics of such actors as Al Jolson, Eddie Cantor, and the black face concepts of Amos and Andy. Gioia, Ted. "Al Jolson: A Megastar Long Buried Under a Layer of Blackface - Jim Crow Museum - Ferris State University". ferris. edu. Retrieved 22 September 2018

Jolson has been dubbed "the king of blackface" performers,[5][6] a theatrical convention since the mid-19th century. With his dynamic style of singing jazz and blues, he became widely successful by extracting traditionally African- American music and popularizing it for European- American audiences who were otherwise not receptive to the originators. [7] Despite his promotion and perpetuation of black stereotypes , [8] his work was sometimes well-regarded by black publications and he has sometimes been credited for fighting against black discrimination on Broadway[5] as early as 1911. In an essay written in the 21st century, Ted Gioia of the Jim Crow Museum of Racist Memorabilia remarked, "If blackface has its shameful poster boy, it is Al Jolson", showcasing Jolson's complex legacy in American society. [9]

End of Article

The fact that African American publications would write favorably about something so degrading to our race, as a White minstrel "performer", is evidence that they were just happy to be included in something that was popular, even if it meant being portrayed in a negative way.

Looking from another angle, there was a mindset in parts of the African American community which felt that, just getting our foot in the door would eventually lead to having a better position at the table. My position is that the popularity and acceptance of minstrel shows helped to perpetuate many of the stereotypes against Black people which are still with us today.

America seems to feel that we, African Americans, should be so thankful for whatever we get that it's ridiculous for us to complain. "Why just 150 years ago you were still a slave." Well either we're all the way free or we're not. There is no, in between. And if you regret what your ancestors did to my ancestors, then treat me equally as *a full citizen* of this country. If you're not regretful, then stop pretending that things are different and admit that you would prefer that I was still a slave and we can at least understand each other and work from an honest position.

As theater developed professionally, and went in a better direction, it prompted local actors to start their own theater workshops within smaller venues having minimal seating capacity. If you couldn't visit Broadway, you could visit your local, "playhouse", as they were, and are still called. This created a more intimate setting, allowing the audience to feel closer to the production in more ways than one. Most actors belonging to a local playhouse come from the same town or city which houses the theater.

Some of the actors from workshops, as these groups of actors are called, have expressed their satisfaction at having the audience almost within touching distance. Some have said that it is good preparation for the Broadway stages and, also, the big screen. Over the years, out of necessity, theater has become more diverse in its content. Knowing which material suited which audiences and regions has always been very crucial to the success, or failure, of local theater.

There is one play that has captured peoples' hearts right across the country. It's called, "Death of A Salesman". Its acceptance has been attributed to the fact that it features a family struggling to make ends meet. Lead by a father who is a traveling salesman. "A Raisin In The Sun," based on the struggles of an urban Black family was one of the most popular plays enjoyed by African American audiences.

Theater allows for *instant feedback* from a live audience, eliciting emotions as diverse as moans, laughter, tears, or shouts of encouragement from those in attendance. President Abraham Lincoln was *assassinated* while *attending* a play, "Our American Cousin", at Ford's Theater in Washington, D.C. His assassin, John Wilkes Boothe was a well-known stage actor and anarchist.

Even as local productions are thriving in their own way, Broadway is still the place to be, with its grand old theaters which are monuments to the fact that they have stood the test of time *and flourished*. Because of the lavishness and expense required to produce a Broadway show, the market has been tested, but came through with resounding success. Broadway, let's face it, belongs mostly to the wealthy. And if they have anything to say about it, don't expect Broadway theaters' demise anytime soon.

The nickname given to the section of Broadway which houses the main theaters is, "The Great White Way". They say the name comes from the fact that it was the first section of Broadway to have electric lights installed. You will scarcely find theaters on Broadway mounting any type of production that appeals to the common people. Although from time to time they do. Just be prepared to spend big money, because what costs a lot to put on, will surely cost a lot to enjoy.

There have been so many successful plays on Broadway that, for fear of leaving out someone's favorite, I won't try to name them. And some Broadway actors, after having success there, have moved on to acting in movies (the Big Screen). Although this is frowned upon by "pure" stage actors.

The movie industry has had a huge hand in the shaping of American culture and thinking. They have set trends in Fashion. Lifted the morale of our troops *and* the people at home, during war times. Influenced politics and pretty much formed their audiences' opinions in a lot of ways. Movies, like plays, are a way to escape the realities of life for a couple of hours at a time and maybe pick up some knowledge while you're at it.

But unlike plays movies can be viewed over and over. Of course, people who prefer plays will tell you that plays are better because you are required to be good enough to nail your parts *live*, every time.

Inflation and outright pirating of films have driven up the price of movies, yet this industry can also claim itself to be not only surviving but thriving.

The movie industry is one of the greatest promotional machines in the world. They start promoting a new movie far in advance of its release date, building anticipation to the point of almost uncontrollable enthusiasm. Because of the budgets that the movie companies have at their disposal, billboards and other expensive ad campaigns are not a problem. When a movie which has already proven itself, comes out with a sequel, it pretty much takes off by word of mouth as much as advertising.

"Batman", "Superman", "Spiderman", "Star Wars", most of the Disney movies, and recently, almost any of the Marvel Comic heroes. Some characters like "Batman" can switch actors playing the lead part and do even better than the previous "Batman". It seems to be because of anticipating the new trappings and gadgets that the movie will feature.

Movies have been known to change lives, in good ways and in negative ways. This means that they can have a certain amount of influence over the minds of some viewers. Which, if someone decides to act on what they see, could be dangerous. As was the case of a mass murderer, who, by no fault of the movie, decided to act out the "Joker" character.

Americans being such capitalist minded people, *at least those with money*, are always looking for ways to make *more money*. And being a society with quickly decaying morals, they often don't care who gets hurt in the deal.

Greedy people and gullible people are never actually far apart, except in their perception of life and opportunity. The reason that I say this is simple if you consider it. A greedy person is always looking for gullible people to take advantage of to get more of whatever he or she wants, which, if not money, is probably something else of a material nature. A gullible person is usually a *trusting* person. That trusting nature is what usually causes them to *be gullible* in the first place. To a person who has never had much, just the *promise* of something that they need can go a long way.

Realizing this, the greedy person paints a lovely picture for his or her "friend", so well that they can visualize it. In fact, because of the *hope* of promise the greedy person might only have to get the picture started and the gullible person is so hyped up on hope that they will finish the vision themselves.

The greedy person's perception of life is, "You create your own opportunities *in whatever way you can. Even if there are some casualties.*" The gullible person's perception of life is, "Since I don't have any wealth, all I need is an opportunity to get with somebody who does, or at least someone who *knows* how to go about getting it. That way we can both prosper." The most hurtful part is when the greedy one gets to their jump-off point and the gullible one is left thinking there's more to come.

After the civil rights struggle in America, and after coming to terms with the murders of its leaders and lead players, came a sense of relief. There was the feeling that America had finally arrived! We had struggled and finally started to turn the corner. In the minds of so many African Americans, this especially seemed true. Being able to travel freely and not have to worry about breaking any laws by just showing up in certain areas, brought a sigh of relief.

But that was only the beginning. In the minds of the ones who had established "Jim Crow" segregation in the first place, a new type of plan was needed. One of the surest ways to kill a peoples' spirit is to build them up with false hope. Tell them that if they fulfill certain obligations, they can have the fruits of their labors. Only to move the stakes, once they've performed as you have asked them to. *First,* You will need to get their attention.

The American establishment has developed a method of starting trends that lead the masses to think the way that they want them to think. As a matter of fact, this country has, for a long time, set most of the trends that the whole world follows. In this respect, the media (film, television, newspapers, magazines, radio, and now internet) plays a huge role in how Americans, and ultimately, the world's thinking is shaped.

During the late 60's through the mid 70's, because of the need for disarming the revolutionary thoughts of Black people, Hollywood began to produce a different style of movie, like none they had ever done before. The thing that made them different was, they were full of Black people, in roles that made them winners and not losers, for a change. Black people were playing the lead roles with most of the White characters playing villainous, despicable roles and being killed or destroyed.

Most of the story lines were about Black people rising up against exploitation of some sort. And winning! Ironically, the movies themselves were exploiting Black people by selling them "fake realities". The White players were cast to be as evil as possible. Giving Black heroes the opportunity to get revenge and be the ultimate winners by the end of the movie.

Many of these types of movies were released during that time. Bringing Black people to the theaters in droves every time a new one was released. In actuality this was a *virtual victory* only. People stepped out of the theaters and right back into the realism of American racism.

The purpose of these "blaxploitation" movies, as they were eventually and accurately described, was to make Black people, especially the young ones, feel good about getting even with their White oppressors. The other purpose was to find out how many Black people, *actually felt* that way.

Many of the lead actors and actresses became *superstars* in the Black community. Some were even referred to, in real life, by their screen names because of lasting impressions that they made on their audiences. Movies like Cleopatra Jones, Shaft, Coffee Brown, Superfly, Blackula, and Sounder. Some of these movies, even though they often made fun of Black people without them realizing it, produced many of the Black community's actors and actresses who were proudly embraced by those in the Black community as their own.

Certain actors are still affectionately referred to by these names, some fifty years later. In case you're wondering why such an impact was made from these movies, it's because Black people were so thirsty to see themselves in a more winning way. Really, just thrilled to see themselves *at all* on the big screen. And these movies provided that. Although in a very *superficial* way. By this I mean that Black heroes were going against organized crime syndicates, killing people who stood in their way, and coming out on top at the end of the movies. Which was not the reality of life as we knew it.

At the core of these movies was an underlying theme of the glamorization of drug dealing, pimping, prostitution, murder and robbery. The likes of which are still, in some ways, thought of as being legitimate means of survival in the Black community "Because that's all we are allowed to do."

They even have pet names for these crimes. Robbery and stealing are referred to as, "hittin' a lick." Probably derived from the past description of a person who wouldn't work, "wouldn't hit a lick at a snake." Pimps and men who have lots of women are now referred to as "players." Which shows a certain amount of respect and admiration.

There were some people connected to these "blaxploitation" movies who used the opportunities as teachable moments. Few, if any, seized the opportunity like Curtis Mayfield, who was a type of prophet in his warnings to those who might allow themselves to be exploited in this manner. When scoring "Superfly", starring Ron O'Neal, a former stage actor, this is very much apparent. Even though the lead character, "Priest", was a drug dealer, Curtis pointed out in the title song, "Superfly", that "a weakness was shown, 'cause his hustle (dealing cocaine) was wrong".

Curtis didn't want the viewers looking up to a drug dealer, no matter how influential the character was in his role. "Don't forget, he's a drug dealer and we are not co-signing that part of this character."

The fact of the matter is, the point was lost on most of the people listening because "hustling" had *already reached* such a level of respect in most urban communities. The role models having the highest visibility and appearing to be the most successful members of the community *were* the "hustlers".

Other songs on the soundtrack also point out the ills of drug dealing and drug consumption. "Freddie's Dead" was another great example of Curtis using the opportunity to write an "anti- soundtrack" and have it come out positive. "A Freddie's on the corner now."
(meaning, although Freddie's dead, another one has taken his place on the corner) "And if you wanna be a junkie, Wow!"

Some of the names hurled at the white characters, and the things that Black people did to them in these movies wouldn't have been tolerated, had it been the other way around. But these were movies and *not* real life. And there was a method to the madness. These movies were meant to *satisfy* Blacks and *enrage* Whites. And it worked. Anything to keep the confrontation between the races going.

It has been said that Hollywood teaches America how to think by influencing the popular opinions of its movie audiences. *Giving* them their opinion. Could this be the case in the Black community? "You see it, now you want to be it." The "blaxploitation" movies could very well have been priming Black America for the influx of drugs, such as powdered cocaine and eventually "crack cocaine", which sifted the Black communities across America like wheat.

If it was intended to destroy *only* Blacks, I don't believe the research was very well thought out. By the time anyone came up for air, "crack" had crossed racial barriers, social and political barriers, class barriers and almost every other type of barrier that you could name.

Even some preachers became hooked on this highly addicting drug. Not even *corporate America* was spared. At this point, the government began to construct programs to deal with the epidemic of crack. Once White America falls into a trap which has been set for Black America it becomes a concern to everyone. "How did this happen?" "What is going on with our society?"

The crack problem in America is reminiscent of the "Opium Wars" which were waged against China back in the 1800's. The big difference is, China's drug wars were waged by *outside forces*, mainly France and Great Britain.

While America's crack cocaine problem is strongly alleged to have been initiated from within our own government. In order to raise arms to assist rebels of a foreign power, in overthrowing a government that wasn't favored by America.

As a Black American, my biggest concern is that Black American citizens could even be *considered* as throw-a-ways by their own government. But it wasn't the first time (the Tuskegee "Experiment", where young Black men were unknowingly used in a syphilis experiment) and won't be the last.

The stereotype that Black Americans are satisfied with not having much, when it comes to realizing the American Dream has long been believed. "Just let them have some music, alcohol, drugs, sex and they're happy." In some ways that might appear to be true for *many* Americans these days. *Regardless* of their race. But this is far from the *real* truth.

Most Americans have just become *used* to making the best of not having much. And that is only because they haven't had a *chance* to have much. They *want* more and are constantly being told that they can have more but are being blocked at every avenue.

The boundaries for achievement are constantly being moved out of reach. Most Americans that I have had the pleasure of knowing, of *any* race, are looking for the same things. The best life that they can provide for themselves and their families, with a fair opportunity to do so.

Another of the games being played in this country is the "blame game". Blame everyone else for your shortcomings. Even the government does it. This type of thinking has become so commonplace that it is stifling a lot of progress by taking away the will of people who feed into it.

If I, as a Black man believed that I couldn't do anything because the "White man" is going to stop me, I wouldn't even be writing this book. Although I *expect* opposition to almost everything that I do, I'm not going to let that *stop* me. *Honestly*, I expect the opposition to come from Blacks, as well as Whites! And for different reasons, but do the reasons *really matter?* Hurdles are hurdles.

Hollywood has, since its beginning, sold its own version of American life to the world and to America itself. And has been so successful at it, that this "dream life" has become the standard by which many people, in America, and around the world, measure their own lives. Often coming up short in the self- esteem department because the bar that they have set for themselves according to the "dream life" is unrealistically high.

Soap operas, another side of Hollywood, have done almost as much, if not more, to influence everyday Americans' lives as the movies have. In fact, people have been so enthralled, and felt such an affinity to some of the characters from soap operas that they even named their children after them.

After realizing how much these shows meant to so many people, the producers found more ways to engage their audiences and increase their profits. Meet and greets became popular, where the "common folks" could come out and rub shoulders with the "stars", as they were now called, and buy pictures and other items of memorabilia to keep them connected to their favorite stars.

All of this seemed to put the "dream life" within reach of the fans. Made them desire to have the same lifestyle as the "rich and famous". Soap operas were known for their attempt at perfection. In household furnishings, clothes worn by the actors and actresses, the make-up and hairstyles of the stars, the way they spoke, and sometimes the way they walked. Even the ashtray on the coffee table was uniquely made. Prompting onlookers to be in awe. "I want one of those"!

Their outfits created fads. Sending women to the stores in droves looking for *that* dress. The one "Erica" wore to "Gloria's" wedding. Even the elderly, had heads of thick, perfectly styled hair. Everyone's fingernails were always ready for a closeup. It was Hollywood, doing what it does best, *selling dreams*. And America doing what it does best, *eating them up*. Hanging on every scene and looking forward to the next time. The need is reciprocal. They need us and we need them. We're being sold a dream, but we're thankful for it because it gives us an escape from reality.

In the meantime, they are looking to give us something even more spectacular the next time. Is there anything wrong with that. Only if we're *rooted* in fantasy, because then we *lose sight of reality*. And reality doesn't fare well, if not tended to. Eight hours of video games and ten minutes of interacting with real people doesn't only "make Jack a *dull boy*", it takes away his social skills and makes him unaware of what is *really* going on.

In America, style has replaced substance. *Style* has become the most important goal, in many peoples' minds. Some are willing to put everything on the line, in order to appear, *in style*. The "dream" has been sold so well, that it left many people feeling inadequate because they couldn't live up to these expectations.

Wives sometimes put their wants ahead of their needs, getting the wants and needs mixed up, priority wise. Husbands might be thought of as not being able to hold up their end of the bargain by not keeping their wives living lavishly, like the soap opera characters.

Some companies realizing the opportunity to fill a need and make a buck, started to produce knock-off items in order to allow the ladies to dress like their favorite stars and have home furnishings like them, as well. That culture, now known as "pop culture," which is the sameness that America revolves around, has taken over our thinking to the point of, sometimes dimming our view of real life. We have become a "whatever is in style" and a "whatever *everybody else* is doing" society.

Pop culture has become the *ruling* culture, and no one seems to mind. We have become so enamored with money and stars that we have even begun to elect them to public offices, on their fame, social and financial statuses alone. People are so taken with stars that a whole industry has been created around "star gazing". Following the ways in which they are living and sometimes even to the point of trying to emulate them. So much so that America's most well received programs are reality shows, observing how the rich and famous live.

The leading trendsetters in pop culture have been leaning heavily on Black inspired attire, music, dance, sports, and popular jargon for quite some time now. All, while ignoring *the source*. Black America.

Too many Black people are so caught up in *"being Black"* that they haven't even noticed that their ideas are being copied and sold back to them in a new package. The latest style of tennis shoe or what is the latest fashion trend are all that is important *to too many people*. While corporate America portrays Black America as buffoons and time wasters, they are, by the same token, using our ideas to feed the pop culture. Just not calling it Black though. "A rose by any other name, is a rose just the same."

The fashion industry is especially guilty of exploiting Black people by observing what is trending in our community, manufacturing it and bringing it out at a price that would make anyone else say that the cost was too high. This (the high price tag) is viewed by many in the Black community as a status symbol. "I bought this, and it makes me *somebody*, because not everyone can afford it." The sad part about it is, *neither can you* afford it. Affording something means being able to buy it without crippling your finances.

Some of us have recognized this exploitation for a while, without being able to do much about it. But things are beginning to change because of Black people, like P. Diddy and some others who have created their own fashion lines. Professional basketball players like Michael Jordan, Lebron James, and Stephen Currie have deals with sneaker companies where they design their own shoes.

However, when a professional basketball player by the name of Stephon Marbury, started a line of clothes and shoes in a price range meant to be affordable to people with ordinary budgets, Black people elected to pay "name brand" prices and not support his product. The reason that they usually offered was, "his brand looks too wack." In my opinion, his products looked great and were a better buy for the money. But knowing my people, I suspect that it is embedded in many Black peoples' brains that everything must be name-brand.

In some strange way, I believe that many African Americans feel that by shopping name-brand, it gives them a better quality of life, making up for many of the other things that are out of reach. Like owning a home and having a decent bank account.

In other words, "If I have to live poor, at least I can spice things up *this way*." The problem with this thinking is the excessive amounts of money spent on buying expensive clothes and shoes could be more wisely spent on trying to *really* change their situation. 500, 400, or 250 dollars for a pair of shoes is, *definitely, excessive*. Unless you're wealthy. And even then, it can be considered decadent.

Some people can be so fashion conscious, and have a desire to look good, that they might cause another person bodily harm to make it possible. And people *have even been killed* in the process of being robbed for the apparel they were *wearing* at the time.

People who *have* money, believe that it is for making *more* money. Those who don't have a lot of money, tend to act like it's just for spending. So, they spend all they get. On *temporary* happiness. Think about this. Would you rather *look like* you have money, or would you rather *have* money?

I know that throughout this conversation, it seems that I have been speaking of African Americans' wasteful spending habits. The truth is, although they are in the majority, when it comes to poor spending habits, this is also true for many White, and other non-Black people who don't have a lot of money.

All of us are being bombarded with advertisements for clothes, televisions, furniture, cars, and so many things that we can't "afford", but can make us feel, and look, like we're doing better than we are. As a result, many have bitten the hook and been left in tremendous debt.

Which brings to mind, the age-old stereotype of a Black man living in a rundown shack, with an expensive car parked out front. In his mind the car represents status. But in the minds of those observing him, it represents ignorance. I wonder if he doesn't feel that he will never be able to afford the payments on a better house, so he spends what money he has, on a car.

Or is he just living for the moment? Enjoying the car and the attention that it brings him. Not realizing that, most of the observers probably consider him a fool instead of marveling at the nice car he possesses.

Regarding the spending habits of poor people. Every spring and summer, they are targeted by manufacturers of cheaply made apparel. Which often comes in the form of poor - quality shoe wear, hats, sunglasses, sundresses.

These items are then, widely promoted as something that the trendy people *must* have, to be "in fashion". Often coming in bright colors. Anything to be different and be seen. Being of poor quality they're usually broken or worn out before summer's over.

I suppose temporary pleasure can be better than none at all. In their own way, poor people are creating a lot of trends that corporate America follows, but not realizing it, and not receiving any of the monetary gains from it.

The majority of people in this country are poor. That constitutes the masses. If you can somehow satisfy the *masses* and *profit* from it, that makes perfect business sense. The only way that they can purchase the product, with money being in short supply, is to make and sell it cheaply. There you have your summer trends. With ideas *brought to you, from you*. And you probably didn't even know it!

Hoola hoops and shower shoes are prime examples of summer trends which caught on in a big way *and lasted*. The difference though, is that both of those items, although cheaply made and affordably priced, were *useful* in their own ways. Hoola hoops were, and still are, a great exercise apparatus. They also provide clean fun for children, as well as adults.

Shower shoes are a mainstay summer wardrobe piece for many people who don't want to wear shoes, but don't want to go barefoot either. They can also be very useful in preventing athletes' foot when showering in public places, such as schools or any place else where people share floor space while going barefoot.

One thing that I have noticed about the attitudes of most Americans is, they get bored so easily. And I believe that it often works against us. If something is working and is beneficial to you, why change it? But we often do. In some countries, they have been doing certain things the same way for ages. Simply because it's working. And they proudly call it *tradition*.

Yet, in America, we are *constantly changing*. Faster, better, stronger. Could it be that the pressure to turn in a stronger performance every time is part of what is causing people to unravel? Because they *are*. And there has to be *some* rational explanation. But real, *honest*, self-examination is becoming harder and harder for America to perform on itself. The reason for that is, we always think of ourselves as being, "the best." *Always*.

"Trading tradition for style"

Funny *Business*

A big part of American pop culture has become the need for laughter, for which people will pay, *and pay well*. But you had better be funny. Or they can break your heart. *Literally*. I wonder though, if the fine line between the *hysterics of life* and hysterical laughter isn't the reason for so much tragedy in the lives of our comedians. So much of the comedy that makes us laugh the hardest, is born of someone's misery. Often the comedians' themselves. I won't use names, but most of us are aware of at least one "tragic comedian".

When I speak of "tragic comedians", I mean no disrespect. After all, how much bad can be said about a person who dedicates their life to making others happy. Maybe if we weren't so *demanding* in our need for laughs, they would have something left for themselves. But *we want it all*. Every time. "Wasn't he, or she funny tonight. Even better than the last time." They know *they'd better be*. Or you would have walked out, compounding their ever-present feeling of teetering on the edge of being a loser, with your walking out and confirming to them that "yes", they are a loser. Once again, such a heavy price to pay for some laughter.

But in defense of being a *successful* comedian, it has its perks. In fact, being a successful comedian means that you sit on a lofty perch among entertainers. Actually, *above* some forms of entertainment. Because egos can be so fragile among entertainers, we won't be specific, but comedy is among the top fields. *Really? Just for making people laugh?!* Um huh. Just for making people laugh. Do you realize how hard that can be? With all of the jokes and ways of looking at situations that have come before, it has to be hard to see something *new* in it and *still be funny*.

And you thought your job was hard. We all have our place in making the wheels turn, so in that respect, *all* jobs are important. But the harder we work, the more we need something to take our minds off of it, with laughter being one of our favorite ways.

I had the pleasure of listening to comedian Dave Chappelle's latest show and I find myself pondering on many of the things that he discussed, because although it was comedy, it was serious in nature. As it has always been, comedy is important to making revolutionary changes to our ways of thinking. Sometimes *reflecting* the changes and sometimes *dictating* them, but like music, always *being a part* of the change in some way.

Imagine how uneventful life would be if there were no music or comedy. Music and comedy are a part of almost every form of entertainment that we hold dear. Most sitcoms are of a comedic form and just like life itself, they vary in their style of comedy to suite different tastes.

Many comedians have gone on to become movie stars because of the fame garnered by their comedy. Their comedic talent has made room for their acting talent, which really do go hand in hand. Their acting skill probably comes with having to move from one character to another during their comedy act.

If you really think about it, comedy has been the route by which quite a few well-known entertainers have entered the industry since the beginning of movie making. Charlie Chaplin is just one example.

Coming later were, Jack Benny and Bob Hope, to name the more successful ones. There was, *and still is*, "gold in them there laughs," if you can connect with the "funny bone." In more recent times there have been Richard Pryor, Eddie Murphy, Robbin Williams, Steve Martin, Chris Rock, and Martin Lawrence. And *most* recently, Kevin Hart. All have become superstars by way of having successful comedy acts first.

CHAPTER 9

Voting Rights...and Wrongs

Probably the most powerful weapon used against the Black citizens of America in modern times is, finding ways to suppress their voting power. Or maybe I should say, limiting their power by finding systemic ways to suppress the Black vote. While trying to make it all *look* legal.

There are numerous ways by which voting rights have been denied to the African American voter. The most blatant way of denying Black people their voting rights was by mobs of Whites turning them away from voting polls in many of the southern states. And this was as recent as post-World War II.

Voting is one of the most important things that a person can do to have an opinion in how they are to be governed. In order to vote, a person must be a citizen of whatever jurisdiction the voting is taking place in. The right to vote is one of those things that people feel so passionate about, that they might even put their lives on the line.

Seeing as how important voting rights are, it's easy to understand why someone who wants to control a situation would want to suppress as many decision-makers as possible, who might oppose them. And the right to vote definitely gives a person their opportunity to be a decision-maker.

America has been, since its declaration, a vote driven country. That's what the Revolutionary War was about. The rights for the newly formed country to govern *themselves* by way of a democratic voting system.

It's understandable that a people who brought a whole other race of people to this country, for the purpose of exploiting them, would not want to turn around and give them voting rights. Especially such a large number of them. But America is a place of contradictions. When it comes to this country's relationship with its African American citizens, it has been filled with a lot of ups and downs. "Now you have it; now you don't". Today they give it; tomorrow they take it away.

The following, is a prime example of the attempts that have been made to try and take away the voting rights of Black men after slavery was abolished in the south. Women had not yet been given the right to vote either.

The following is an excerpt taken from:
Constitutional Rights Foundation, 601 S.Kingsley © 2019 CRF-USA.ORG Dr., Los Angeles, CA 90005, 213.487-5590 F 213. 386-0459

Website: https://www.crf-usa.org/brown-v-board-50th-anniversary/race-and-voting.html

Voting During Reconstruction

After the Civil War, Congress acted to prevent Southerners from re-establishing white supremacy. In 1867, the Radical Republicans in Congress imposed federal military rule over most of the South. Under U.S. Army occupation, the former Confederate states wrote new constitutions and were readmitted to the Union, but only after ratifying the 14th Amendment. This Reconstruction amendment prohibited states from denying "the equal protection of the laws" to U.S. citizens, which included the former slaves.

In 1870, the 15th Amendment was ratified. It stated that, "The right of citizens of the United States to vote shall not be denied or abridged by the United States or by any State on account of race, color, or previous condition of servitude."

More than a half-million black men became voters in the South during the 1870s (women did not secure the right to vote in the United States until 1920). For the most part, these new black voters cast their ballots solidly for the Republican Party, the party of the Great Emancipator, Abraham Lincoln.

When Mississippi rejoined the Union in 1870, former slaves made up more than half of that state's population. During the next decade, Mississippi sent two black U.S. senators to Washington and elected a number of black state officials, including a lieutenant governor. But even though the new black citizens voted freely and in large numbers, whites were still elected to a large majority of state and local offices. This was the pattern in most of the Southern states during Reconstruction.

The Republican-controlled state governments in the South were hardly perfect. Many citizens complained about overtaxation and outright corruption. But these governments brought about significant improvements in the lives of the former slaves. For the first time, black men and women enjoyed freedom of speech and movement, the right of a fair trial, education for their children, and all the other privileges and protections of American citizenship. But all this changed when Reconstruction ended in 1877 and federal troops withdrew from the old Confederacy.

Voting in Mississippi

With federal troops no longer present to protect the rights of black citizens, white supremacy quickly returned to the old Confederate states. Black voting fell off sharply in most areas because of threats by white employers and violence from the Ku Klux Klan, a ruthless secret organization bent on preserving white supremacy at all costs.

White majorities began to vote out the Republicans and replace them with Democratic governors, legislators, and local officials. Laws were soon passed banning interracial marriages and racially segregating railroad cars along with the public schools.

Laws and practices were also put in place to make sure blacks would never again freely participate in elections. But one problem stood in the way of denying African Americans the right to vote: the 15th Amendment, which guaranteed them this right. To a great extent, Mississippi led the way in overcoming the barrier presented by the 15th Amendment.

In 1890, Mississippi held a convention to write a new state constitution to replace the one in force since Reconstruction. The white leaders of the convention were clear about their intentions. "We came here to exclude the Negro," declared the convention president. Because of the 15th Amendment, they could not ban blacks from voting. Instead, they wrote into the state constitution a number of voter restrictions making it difficult for most blacks to register to vote.

- END OF ARTICLE

When America declared itself democratic in the eyes of the world, it gave itself a philosophy to live up to. As every observer can see, it *appears* and claims to be, the world's most democratic country, but with a lot of shortcomings and a very long way to go before it lives up to its name. Mass incarceration of Black people, particularly males, are always at a disproportionately high level, when compared to any other race of people in America.

In many states by committing a felony, you forfeit your right to vote. Because of this, felonies are charged to Black males as frequently as possible. This is used to cut down on the Black community's voting power.

St. Louis, Missouri, of which, Ferguson is a suburb, is a case in study of Black men being overcharged with crimes, for the sake of raising revenue.

AN ARTICLE FROM: THIS STORY WAS PUBLISHED IN THE NOVEMBER/DECEMBER 2014 ISSUE OF COLUMBIA JOURNALISM REVIEW.WRITER: Lawrence Lanahan

In a piece called "Why the Fires in Ferguson Won't End Soon," Slate's Jamelle Bouie widened the lens even further, addressing other divisive practices such as unequal policing, school segregation, and subprime loan targeting. Bouie, Coy, Balko, and other journalists who addressed the structure behind the St. Louis region's racial divide share one thing in common: They relied on the work of historian Colin Gordon, whose *Mapping Decline: St. Louis and the Fate of the American City* lays out the local policies and practices through which whites were able to isolate themselves residentially from African-Americans over the past 100 years. Gordon says segregation stems partly from Missouri's lax requirements for creating municipalities. "You have six houses and a signature?" Gordon says. "Fine. You're a town!"

- END OF ARTICLE

Ferguson, Missouri was also found (by way of a federal investigation) to be racially profiling African American motorists, excessively, for the purpose of raising badly needed revenue for the city. As noted by Mr. Lawrence Lanahan in his article the one thing that the more fair-minded journalists are beginning to mention is, these things didn't just begin overnight, it *is America's way*. Beginning right after slavery until the present time, a new type of institutionalized racism was felt to be needed and was indeed, instituted.

And it runs deep into the very fabric of America. Albeit, as quietly and secretly as possible. The reason being, most of it is illegal, according to the Constitution and other national laws. These practices are so subtle that you can feel them being implemented but still not be able to put your finger on them. Besides that, the average person is so busy just trying to survive and get along without complicating their lives that they will tolerate more than they really care to. Just trying to keep the peace.

Since, during the 2016 presidential election, the outcome was determined by the electorate college vote, while the popular vote was won by the opposing candidate, many people are under the impression that their, one person, one vote doesn't count anymore.

That is setting a very dangerous precedent. One which we cannot afford to buy into. As African Americans, we must always be aware of the people who suffered, and even died for our right to vote. For that reason, we *must* vote. And we *must* keep the channels open, *at any cost.*

Knowing that our right to vote can be taken away by being convicted of certain legal offenses, we have to avoid committing those infractions. That is, if we are serious about our right to vote. There is such a thing as your rights being taken away *and* such a thing as *giving* your rights away.

Weaker and Wiser

When I was a child of the 50's there was a saying among the older Black people, "This world is growing weaker and wiser." With me being a studious child, who felt I was smarter than these " old folks", I thought, surely, they mean, "wickeder and wiser". This, in my mind meant that the world is growing more wicked and are smarter about how they are doing it. Defeating themselves through their own wisdom. As the years passed, and I grew older myself, I realized that the old folks knew exactly what they were saying.

I now believe they meant that the world is getting weaker, in the ways of morality, and too smart for their own good. Meaning that people are outsmarting themselves in their self-absorbed wisdom and loss of morals.

When you look around, it's obvious that the morals of America, as well as other countries, are slipping far below what they once were, even what they were a few years ago.

Things like murder seeming to be easier for people to commit without feeling remorse. There are men who feel that raping a female is alright if she has "lead them on." *Eliminating all witnesses* seems to be a good enough reason to kill someone who has seen you commit a crime. This is thought to be "good thinking," by some people who commit crimes.

To a criminal-minded person, committing a crime in a certain manner can sometimes make them feel *smarter*. When, actually, committing a crime in the first place *says you're not smart*.

But society has begun to romanticize some types of criminal activity because of how they have been desensitized by the movie and television industries.

Bank robbers, in particular, are sometimes viewed as heroic because they're seen as robbing those who are robbing others. They are said to be treated with a certain amount of respect in the prison system. Bankers are thought of as being ruthless, by many, because of how they foreclose on loans and debts of people who can't afford to keep up their payments.

At some point in their life, many people have been in contact with bankers for one reason or another and had an unflattering outcome. Whether it was an unsuccessful attempt to secure a loan or being foreclosed on a home, banks are known to be unrelenting, as they are required to be, if they intend to stay in business. But to the public, at large, and sometimes rightfully so, they're seen as villains. So, almost anyone who deals a blow to this group is thought of, by many, as doing everyday people, a favor.

CHAPTER 10

A New Song

The music industry has, for quite some time, played a major role in the shaping of America. And vice versa. Music imitated life, and life imitated music. Even before it could be called an industry, music was influencing the way people were viewing, and experiencing life in this country. That's where the gospel, blues, country, and jazz forms of music were derived from. Life itself. However, as the nation grew and prospered, a certain amount of *fantasy* was factored into the music. A type of fantasy that allowed us to portray life the way we *wanted* to see it. Not the way it actually *was*.

Black peoples' contribution to the shaping of music in America got its start from the cotton fields of the south, in the form of "field hollers." These were chants that the field workers would perform among themselves to pass the time and lighten the workload. Passing chants back and forth about different subject matter. Sometimes about their working situations and sometimes about their relationships. It depended on what caught the interest of the participants and those listening.

Then came the negro spirituals. Accepting the religion of the slaveowners as their own, they began to sing the songs of the Christian faith with an interpretation that was uniquely their own. Incorporating "field hollers" and dance. Using different, more upbeat, rhythms with hand clapping. From these origins, the music of African Americans began to branch out in different directions.

During the 20's and 30's "race music," the name given to *any type* of Black music, began to be recorded by Black artists and sold within the Black community. The only place that it was *allowed* to be sold. Once the word got around, young White people began to buy these records and listen to them, without their parents knowing about them venturing into this forbidden area and buying music which would *"surely corrupt them."*

This music came in the form of blues, jazz, ragtime (which *spawn* jazz), rhythm & blues and gospel. All of these types of music were developed by African Americans, combining the vocals and rhythms of the Western region of the African continent with European instruments and musical scales. *All* of the styles of music that were developed in America, after these forms, owe a great debt to the forerunners.

While the music couldn't erase the fact that the lynching of Black people was taking place, the blues and gospel gave a sort of sad comfort to those suffering under these conditions. What started as sad and mournful idioms of music, would then begin to include songs about love and hope. Since, from the days of slavery, most Africans were not allowed to play the music or sing the songs from their own countries, they came up with new forms of music which appealed to Blacks *and* Whites.

GOSPEL

In need of something that would give them hope, Black people turned to the spiritual side of life. The heartfelt music of their new religion. The only other music which came even close to being as emotional as gospel music, was the blues. This gospel music could make people cry, shout, scream and pass out in the Spirit. Gospel music became the "pop music" of the African American community. I say that because of its popularity.

There were some households where the blues could not be played because they were considered too explicit. L

Blue lyrics were often very sexual in nature. And in most Christian families, secular music of *any* type was not allowed.

The gospel quartets began singing on circuit tours and were treated royally by their followers. The quartets became so famous that, years later, they would be the inspiration for secular groups like the Temptations.

Almost every rhythm and blues singer, years later, would claim a well-known gospel singer as the person that they adapted their singing style from. The gospel artists, especially the male quartets, were the Black community's first "superstars." Wherever they went, during the seasons *when people had money to spend on tickets*, they would be treated like royalty. Being fed home cooked meals by the church sisters.

Because of the lack of hotels, where they were *allowed* to sleep, they would often be taken in by the local church people while in town, as they saturated the southern states with gospel tours.

James Cleveland held his own as a solo gospel singer, writing many of his own songs and usually traveling with his choir. Female groups, which were more like small choirs, were much in demand also. Groups like Clara Ward and the Ward Singers, The Caravans, who gave us Albertina Walker, Dorothy Norwood, Inez Andrews, and the renown Shirley Caesar. All solo singers in their own right.

The most famous *family* group was The Staple Singers, featuring Roebuck "Pop" Staple and Mavis Staple on lead. Mavis could sing so deep I would call it bass. With a family style of harmony all their own.

But most of the adoration of the women of the churches was saved for the men of the quartets. Groups like The Dixie Hummingbirds, The Blind Boys of Mississippi, The Blind Boys of Alabama, and The Soul Stirrers which, eventually featured Sam Cooke.

Gospel music has been and still is a staple of the Black community. Sunday morning is gospel music time in many African American homes, as many people prepare to go to church. Gospel music was a staple of the Civil Rights movement, as well. It is and will always be an important part of African American lives.

HIT PARADE

During the 50's and early 60's "Hit Parade" radio stations played everything from, jazz, country, blues, to rhythm and blues, all from the same charts. By the *late* 60's, stations started to specialize in *one* type of music as opposed to blending everything together. Of course, you *always* had the stations that specialized in the different types of music, but it wasn't quite the same as when you could listen to them *all on one station*.

JAZZ

Jazz music is regarded as America's own form of classical music. Not to be confused with the European form of classical music, but classic in style and content. Jazz, as it is simply called, is to this day, the most sophisticated form of music ever completely *originated* in America.

The creation of jazz was shared by many, who dedicated their lives, *literally*, to the evolution of it. The pioneers of jazz spent countless hours, sometimes not sleeping for days, perfecting this new music. Taking instruments invented in Europe and using them in ways, which previously, had never been done. People like John Coltrane, Charlie Parker, Miles Davis, Duke Ellington, and Dizzy Gillespie spent years, vigorously and with a deep respect, figuring out and perfecting the intricacies of jazz.

Since its inception jazz has fascinated the world. So much so that it is still taught, dissected, and appreciated as a major art form by many music enthusiasts. Various colleges and universities throughout the world, offer courses in elaborate jazz studies. Still breaking down and learning to understand what the masters of the idiom have left us, in such a rich legacy of music.

As jazz grew more popular, it produced even more genres of itself, with White jazz artists entering the fray playing their own interpretations. When this happened, even *Hollywood* got involved. Placing jazz musicians in some of their mainstream movies. Mostly White artists like Glenn Miller, but sometimes Black jazz artists too. Like Count Basie, Louis Armstrong, and Louis Jordan.

Jazz artists generated styles of dress because they were *expected* to be well groomed and well-dressed to set them apart from their audiences. And they rose to the occasion. Jazz artists came decked out in wide- lapel suits with baggy, pleated pants. Wide multi-patterned neckties, two-tone shoes and wide-brimmed hats.

Since everyone worked, or "hustled", hard for their money, they expected you to perform and look like you were worth them spending their money on. And because the club goers were sharp dressers themselves, the "stars" had to be a cut above them, giving them something to broaden their style scope and possibly emulate. Two of the standout artists of that genre were Miles Davis, trumpeter, (who had his clothes tailormade) and Cab Calloway, band leader, who helped to popularize the zoot suit.

When the fashion was right and the music was "tight", the stage was set for a great "jam session". What took place was something called, "cutting heads", where the best musicians would compete against each other on their respective instrument. Letting the audience decide who "cut" who's head, musically. This required much practice and preparation, in order to be ready to shine.

What resulted is some of the most intricate music ever developed on American soil. Many jazz musicians poured their heart and soul into their music. There was also a camaraderie between them whereby they shared their new musical discoveries among themselves.

The downside of jazz is that it literally killed many of its pioneers *because of that same dedication to the art form*. Many of them hardly slept at all. Many were heavily into some type of drugs, or alcohol. Anything to keep them in a creative spirit. The stories of their deaths are well-known. Their musical legacies and contributions live on in others who have taken up the mantle, but with a more discretionary approach. People like the Marsalis Brothers, Wynton and Branford.

COUNTRY

I would be remiss not to include that other American original, country music. Country music owes a lot to jazz *and* blues and from its beginnings leaned heavily on regional folklore, combined with music which reminded them, as much as possible, of the "old country". A large number of early country songs were bright and hopeful. Celebratory in tone.

Then country songs began to reflect the realities of life. Love and heartbreak became the central theme of country music. Unlike jazz, which mostly didn't include many lyrics from the beginning, Country was as much about the stories as about the music.

Artists such as Patsy Cline, George Jones, Hank Williams Sr., Eddie Arnold, Hank Snow (a Canadian), Little Jimmie Dickens, Bill Monroe and many others, brought country music, front and center right across America.

Southern by origin, but nationally accepted, country music became the music that many White Americans, and to be completely honest, quite a few African Americans, embraced in a major way. It was a style whose central theme was storytelling, married to a type of *music* that tugged at your emotions.

The name, country music, is really a shorter version of the name that it was originally called by. *Country and Western*. And although the "western" part of the name has been left off, some of the earlier country artists are famous for their western style dressing. Not just *any* cowboy look, but the fanciest type of western look you can imagine. Colors, styles, and materials all came together to produce the outfits that made country artists stand out from all others.

Male and female country artists pretty much dressed alike, except, of course, the men wore pants and the women, skirts and dresses. The same thing applied as it did in jazz music or any other type, you had to be sharper than your audience. *And they were.*

I've heard country artists talk about wearing outfits so heavily decorated with adornments like beads and metal that they could barely get through their show. But they looked spectacular!

*The following article is taken from the website below.

https://www.wideopencountry.com/country-fashion-trends/

The Best and Worst Country Fashion Trends in History

BY BOBBIE JEAN SAWYER 1 YEAR

In the early days of country music, most singers opted for a more casual style to relate to the common man and woman. The Carter Family wore simple dresses and suits. Kitty Wells wore gingham dresses favored by 1950s homemakers. Then Nudie Cohn came along. Inspired by design pioneers Nathan Turk and Rodeo Ben, the Russian-born Cohn revolutionized country music fashion with his elaborate <u>Nudie suits</u>. Adorned with rhinestones and extravagant embroidery, the suits were flashy enough to make a singer stand out from a mile away.

Country artists couldn't get enough. Porter Wagoner, Hank Williams and countless other stars clamored for Nudie's eye-catching designs.

- **End of Article**

Though country artists' tastes in fashion have been simplified over the years, people did, and still do, look to country music for storytelling. If there is no storyline, it just doesn't seem like it's country. Over time, the stories have been adapted to suite the changes in lifestyles. As in most other areas of music that have lyrics, the message has turned toward things having to do with sex.

Of course, a theme of sex is nothing new to popular forms of music, but what *is new* is the way in which things are being said. Although country music is by no means, the only form of music which has loosened the "guidelines", so to speak, it was one of the last ones *expected* to do so.

ROCK AND ROLL

Which brings us to what has been called one of the two musical styles to have brought the biggest changes to America's *status quo*. Rock and roll. America has never been the same since the introduction of rock and roll. This music, while in a category of its own, originated from combining *all* of the music which came before it. And shook up the whole world. Blues, jazz, and country were put in a melting pot and came out as rock and roll.

This form of music, originating in the 50's and still developing today, created *many types* of revolutions. For the first time in America, people of different races openly gathered under the same musical umbrella. Sometimes in the same venues. And that did not go unnoticed. There were police at every major rock and roll concert trying to keep the races from mingling together in the concert halls. But eventually the young people won.

Although Little Richard and Chuck Berry, two of the founders of rock and roll, got things started, it soon became *everybody's music*. Jerry Lee Lewis and eventually Elvis Presley helped to give it the "crossover" appeal, making it okay for the White teenagers to like it.

Fact is, they were already "digging" it. But, after a losing battle, waged by their parents, they *completely* embraced rock and roll from any artist that played it well, regardless of race.

Rock and roll changed the way people dressed, talked, walked, and thought. It brought with it a type of rebellious freedom of which America had never experienced, prior to that. And it came with a momentum which couldn't be stopped. No matter how hard they tried to. And they tried pretty hard.

While grownups hated it *at first*, teenagers and young adults, loved it. Rock and roll, a "good time" music, stubbornly, just would not go away. Eventually some of the grown folks got on board, as well. Like Jerry Lee Lewis sang, there was "a whole lot of shakin' going on."

Artists like Buddy Holly and Ritchie Valens, who perished in the same plane crash, introduced some great ballads to what had started out as fever pitch music. "True Love Ways" (Holly) and "Donna" (Valens). Both were known for uptempo rock and roll, as well. This genre of music that swept across America, and the world, left lasting impressions until this day.

Even the name "rock music" evolved from "rock and roll." Groups like the Beatles were direct descendants of "rock and roll" with a blues influence. Blue jeans, bobby sox, penny loafers, white and black oxford shoes, and argyle sweaters were some of the fashions that became popular as part of the rock and roll culture.

Rock and roll introduced sexual songs to the mainstream listeners, mostly by way of, thinly veiled, inuendo. With the bulk of the blame being placed on Black people *"for turning White people into the same crass people that they (Blacks) were."*

Songs like the afore mentioned "Whole Lot of Shakin' Going On", by Jerry Lee Lewis, "Tutti Frutti" by Little Richard, "Shake, Rattle, and Roll," by Big Joe Turner, and "Sixty Minute Man", by The Dominoes. Thus, starting a sexual and cultural revolution, which continues. One important thing rock and roll has proven, is what a powerful tool music can be.

RHYTHM & BLUES

Even though rock and roll had its share of Black artists, they soon began to break away into a style of music which, unlike rock and roll, was dominated by mostly Black artists. This music, which had been emerging since *before* rock and roll, became officially known as "rhythm and blues." Originally performed by some of the Black artists from rock and roll and others, anxious to usher in a style that was more authentic to who *they* were.

However, because *songwriting* was becoming such a lucrative market, in the beginning stages of "r & b", which it was now called, many of the writers were White, with the record companies not giving the Black artists the opportunity to make the kind of money which songwriting generated. Even Black artists who wrote their own songs, most often had their songwriters' royalties and publishing stolen by the heads of the record companies.

As a result of how the White writers perceived Black people to be, many of the records were silly little ditties without any serious meaning. Thankfully, there were also some *great* writers, like Teddy Randazzo, an Italian American who wrote most of Little Anthony and The Imperials' songs, such as, "Tears On My Pillow," " Hurts So Bad," and "Going Out Of My Head".

Very beautiful and intelligently written songs with brilliant arrangements, topped off with spectacular performances by Little Anthony and the imperials. This was, definitely, a sophisticated "uptown New York sound". After listening to Mr. Randazzo's own recordings of his songs, I realize that he had a nice singing voice himself.

On the female side, there was Carole King and her future husband, Gerry Goffin writing, "Will You Still Love Me Tomorrow?", by the Shirelles. Ms. King later had a best-selling album, "Tapestry", on which she wrote and recorded as the artist. The Shirelles are credited with paving the way for the "girl groups", (as they were called), which came after them. They had a number of well-crafted and respected hits which crossed racial barriers. Coming before Motown Records.

But this was an idea which set in motion the desire for more of the same. Motown had studied the "blueprint" and decided to expand upon it.

By the time Motown came on the scene, everything was already primed and waiting for the takeover. And they dominated the rhythm and blues scene to the point that it was pop music really, because of its popularity and the sales that it generated. With Aretha Franklin and Wilson Pickett busting out on Atlantic Records, Detroit artists were on top of the charts and the world.

The decision makers of America have a way of pretending to be taking the country in the direction in which the *masses* desire to go, while, *dictating* that direction *as often as they can.*

HIP HOP

Around 1979, the industry was caught off guard when a new form of popular music was ushered in by a trio of young African American males calling themselves the Sugarhill Gang. Hailing from Englewood, New Jersey, they took their name from a section of Harlem, New York.

The label on which they debuted, was also called Sugarhill Records, owned by Sylvia and Joe Robinson, and administered by their son, Joe Jr. Sylvia, being the same Sylvia, from the duo of Mickey & Sylvia, who had a hit with, "Love Is Strange," a Bo Diddley penned song, which reached the Billboard Pop Chart in 1957. And later, recording "Pillow Talk," as simply, Sylvia.

This style of music performed by the Sugarhill Gang became known as "rap music", for the simple fact, it was spoken words over a beat. It became the first "new" style of music since rock and roll. The big difference was that the song, "Rapper's Delight", was spoken, and not sung. Which was something altogether new. Records had been made before using spoken word, but not with the staccato rhythms used by this new and fresh song.

With the success of "Rapper's Delight" came the need for more of the same. The young people, of all races, embraced rap music and a culture sprang up around it, much like what happened with rock and roll. Only stronger, and with longer lasting results. Rap music started a revolution that began around 1979 and is still evolving today.

Although the genre has transformed from being called, "rap" to being referred to as "hip hop", it still began with "Rapper's Delight." Because it came as such a free form of music, the guidelines were pretty much dictated by the, mostly, young people involved with it. Most grownups *hated it*. Which made the young people love it that much more. They had finally developed something of their own. Something that most grownups could only watch with disgust.

Eventually, with the passing of time, the earlier generation of rap fans grew up. Yet unlike many genres of music where growing up means growing away from things of your youth, hip hop fans stayed loyal to their music.

This produced forty-year old men, who are still saggin'. Which is a big part of the hip hop culture. Wearing their pants below their buttocks, with their underwear exposed. Still "bumping" hip hop from their cars, with bone-shaking and even home-shaking frequencies.

Seeing the opportunity to make as much money as possible from this new music, the recording industry quickly gravitated to hip hop, seeking to use it in more ways than one.

While making money is always front and center, they found a way to use this music as a political tool, as well. Some of the pioneers of hip hop started to use it as a means of teaching cultural awareness to the youth (KRS 1, Public Enemy, Grand Master Flash and the Furious Five).

Then music industry heads started to sway it in the direction of a new genre of hip hop designated as "gangster rap." And for the most part, those not generating gangster rap were not getting signed to recording deals. So, while the relationship between record companies and young hungry artists has always been, "Do as I say, keep your mouth shut and everything will be alright," gangster rap was the order of the day.

There is a story floating around about a record executive who was called to a meeting consisting of the who's who of the record industry. Upon arrival, he noticed some people who were strangers to him. After the meeting got underway, they were told that these people were in the business of building prisons and jails. "What does that have to do with us?" "I 'm glad you asked. We are going to help them by filling their institutions after bringing out a style of music called, gangster rap." He said he then heard a few people who were disgusted by the idea, but he also heard some say, "That'll keep them @$&&#%! in their place."

Since I haven't found any real proof of this anywhere, I can't confirm its authenticity. But we can all attest to the destruction that gangster rap has caused in the Black community. We can look away and say, "I don't see what all of the fuss is about." But we *know* the truth.

The system at work in America, whose aim is to destroy Black America is always looking for ways to get it done, while using *us to do it,* as often as possible. And if we are naïve and money hungry, *or just plain hungry* enough to do it, then who is really to blame? Think about it. "You used me to destroy myself." *Then I have no one to blame but me.* Though you whisper self-destruction in my ear, it is my responsibility not to heed it.

I am aware that not a lot of gangster rap is selling, these days, but I am very aware of the damage which has *already been done.* And I would like to thank everyone who has *refused* to participate and everyone who *stopped* participating in it. I know how hard it is for *anyone*, and especially an African American to provide for ourselves and our families.

At this point I want to look on the brighter side of what hip hop has done for the African American community. We now have Black people who have built empires from the proceeds and gains that hip hop has afforded them. Congratulations to every one of you.

Just know that I don't trust the System and what it will do to you. It will pretend to be your friend and use you against yourself and others like you. *When they start holding you up as an example of whom we should all be like. That's maybe not the best place to be. We will know who you are by the things that you do to further our cause. And if you miss a step. Get right back in line and we promise not to throw you away. We're all in this struggle together.*

"Here's what you *need* to know"

CHAPTER 11

Prepped to Accept

Instinctively, animals *and* humans know when one of their kind is weak, and they seek to *exploit* that weakness. With *people*, the intended gain is most often of a financial or material nature. Once weakness has been spotted, it becomes a target. The more areas of weakness, the more areas to target. From my observation, the Black community has been, and continues to be targeted, and bombarded in *many* ways. One of the most prominent areas of weaknesses is hopelessness. The feeling of hopelessness has made it easy for the Black community to be exploited in so many ways it would be very hard to number them all.

But let's start with the most obvious means. Alcohol and drugs. These are two prime examples of the things that are used in an effort to escape from hopelessness, and those peddling them are doing a thriving business among Black people. Truth is. These things only *add to the individual's downward spiral* bringing about even more hopelessness along with the financial burden that they then place on the users, their families, and loved ones. They don't just *pull* you down, they *keep* you down, and once you're in that state, it's hard to break the cycle.

In what community, other than a poor community, are liquor stores allowed to be so plentiful? After all, they do require licenses, to operate legally. So, obviously the government is complicit, at least on *that* level, because they are the ones who issue the liquor licenses. If they had the community's best interest at heart, there wouldn't be nearly as many licenses issued.

But the only sincere interest, it seems, that *anyone* doing business in the Black community has, is to make money from whatever they can peddle. Then, invest that money elsewhere. Drugs and alcohol being the number one best sellers.

Alcohol is even *advertised* differently in predominately Black areas than in other areas. There are alcoholic beverages which are sold *only* in liquor stores located in *Black* communities. For instance, the malt liquors and beers with the highest alcohol content, are pushed more strongly in the Black neighborhoods than anywhere else. And with very little resistance. I have heard of cases where the store owners, when questioned about how they are exploiting the community, will say, "We help to keep the community running." Yes. Running to the liquor store. There are better ways to get tax money.

And it appears that a large majority of those on the outside looking in, could not care less. "It's not *my* problem". What many people who live outside of predominately Black areas seem to forget is, the Black problem is *everyone's problem*. My reasoning is this; we, in America, are like one big body, wherein if anyone is suffering or ill, the whole body is suffering or soon will be. It might be less obvious at first, but as time goes by it is becoming more apparent.

It's not as simple as, *"Look how they're pulling the country down."* The stereotypes have been *promoted*. And for different reasons. At first, it was for trying to make the rest of society dislike Black people. But the negativity *caught on* and *became hip*. Suddenly, everyone's child wanted to act Black and do the things that young Black people do. It caught on so well that if you closed your eyes it's hard to figure out if the person speaking is Black or White. And that has *incensed* the "Machine" which created it, or at least allowed it to happen.

They never dreamed that the very part of "Blackness" that they hate the most would catch fire and burn them in such a way that it's irreversible, and seemingly, here to stay. They went looking for a way to bring Black people down and got caught in the whirlpool. And America is probably the most structured country in the world.

By that I mean, probably because of a slave past, there are so many rules and regulations in place. You can't do this in such and such a state. But, because there are so many networks in place, trends spread more rapidly. For that reason, it's easy for things to get passed around. And Blackness is a trend that is here to stay. The only problem is, it's not our best work that is on display. We would prefer that the *positive* side of Blackness be displayed.

If America is ever going to be, who it claims to be, there will have to be more attention given to its common people, who have been, for a long time now, neglected and left out of *the total equation*. The mentality has always been to manage the situation of dissatisfaction and unrest by using heavy-handed policing. It's easy to see that's not working.

Preying on the lack of awareness because of the lack of reading and comprehension, politicians have also begun to stoop to new levels of exploitation for gaining votes and controlling the masses. Such as playing up the differences between the races and causing division when they are not really a fan of either group. And seemingly not caring about what the friction leads to.

We have arrived at a point in this country where it has become hard to determine what is lies and what is truth. And the result is a major disconnection between so many factions of people who decide to follow certain differing opinions. Many people, these days, base *their* opinions on the opinions of others, whom they respect, without any further research.

This is happening more often, as time goes by, because Americans are becoming more illiterate and people either *can't* read or *choose not to*. So many have become "surface people". People who only see the surface, without digging any deeper.

This presents a dangerous problem when not *all* of the information has been presented. And if you can't read the only thing that you can do is *guess at what's right or what's wrong* or accept someone else's opinion about it.

To further complicate matters, school officials have decided not to teach cursive writing anymore, because they have deemed it, no longer necessary. The problem with this is, so many things, which are a part of our past, will be lost to the younger generations because of their inability to read cursive writing.

People will no longer be able to personalize their signatures. Old handwritten letters and autographs will be lost to time. In a way, it is an attempt to destroy a part of our past. Which only helps those trying to hide the truth. Their reasoning is, "It's not necessary anymore."

The Constitution and other important documents are written in cursive. The excuse given is, that everything will be *archived* in printed form. The problem with that is, someone must transcribe the information, and can we trust them to be honest and complete? What about old family letters and notes left as heirlooms?

It seems as if, everyone wants to know something that someone else doesn't know and are more than happy to exploit the fact. Authority is coveted by many, and for all the wrong reasons. Where people used to want to bring others along, being privileged to the same knowledge as themselves, they now want to be the *only one* in the know. Which seeks to put the information in the hands of a few, keeping the rest ignorant.

But many seem to be *satisfied* with being ignorant or else they would seek knowledge. Maybe some are even *unaware* that they *are* ignorant. After all, the *meaning of ignorance* is, not knowing.

A person who wishes to get things done will hear the alarm go off, *get up* and go about their business. While a person who doesn't care will hear the alarm go off, *turn it off*, and go back to sleep.

Sometimes with encouragement from people they trust, people can, and do, change. So, don't give up on, and stop encouraging people that you care about. They *need* you. *We* need you. Because until they wake up *and get up*, we are carrying their share of the weight. Which manifests itself in many ways.

When I considered how African Americans have been used and exploited over the years, since slavery, I have realized that it began with the exploitation of the mind. With the demise of slavery, we were not as subjected to *physical exploitation* as we once were. After all, our bodies finally belonged to *us*. This meant that our oppressor had to find new and subtle ways to use us.

What better way than teach you how to program *yourself* negatively? To do this, they used the "shinny beads" trick. Made it look good to the eyes. It is said that the eyes are the gateway to the soul.

For example, by the time the graphics and marketing departments put their touch on a pack of cigarettes, even with the label stating (in bold letters) that this product can cause cancer, the rest of the package looked so good that you could hardly *wait* to smoke one.

And even though that first cigarette was not such a great experience, what with the coughing, dizziness, and nausea, you still went back to try it once more. Probably not realizing that you were preparing yourself to accept something that would only have a negative effect on you. Or maybe you *did* realize and just couldn't help yourself.

We are constantly being programed for whatever assault is coming next. Without knowing it. One important thing is to make sure that anyone who would contest it, doesn't get the memo. That way they can say, "Oh, I thought you knew about it. *Everyone else did.*"

The process of *forcing* change is made easier when the general public are not *expecting* a change. Catching them unprepared and off guard works in favor of the ones implementing the change. They don't want you disrupting things.

You're only told about the part that looks beneficial to you, *if you're told at all.* The other part is kept secret until they've got you thinking favorably about the first part. Like, "Oh we're bringing in a new superintendent of schools. And *he's a Harvard graduate.*" That's meant to impress you. But what they don't tell you is that he's been run out of every district in the neighboring state for unsuccessfully trying to push through the same agenda that they are bringing him to your district to implement.

Everything is being made more difficult in order to keep as *many* as possible, knowing *as little* as possible. For instance, the "new math", which they've made so complicated that, if a parent or guardian hasn't attended school recently, is impossible to understand and assist the student with. Now I pose this question. Does that sound like a situation in which they want you to succeed?

But we have come to a point where they no longer need *your* approval to set the wheels in motion. Remember that last election that you didn't participate in? Well this was on the ballot and since they knew that people like you don't usually vote, that is when they pushed it through. See, the people who don't think the same way as you, the ones who believe everything that the establishment says. *They vote.* Go to the polls like sheep to the pasture. But then that's exactly what they are. Sheep.

Before you know anything about what's going on, the deed has been done and you're standing there feeling confused. Whose fault is it, really? This *is* still America. Your vote still counts, in most instances.

Have you ever had someone do something for you, seemingly, out of the goodness of their heart? Someone whom you have never been able to trust in the past, who now makes you wonder if you were just too hard on them in the first place. Only to find out after accepting the favor, that they want an even *bigger* favor from *you*. Something that you now feel obligated to do.

That's how I feel, being an American, these days. We're not in control of much, *and even that little bit is being snatched away*. With ignorant fellow citizens saying, " Stop your whining. Everything is fine.*" Not realizing they're in trouble too*. When people become complacent and satisfied with just sitting around in their house slippers, remote in hand, watching the news on a superficial level, having no opinion of their own, they are just what the government can use.

And they do. By somehow making them feel that the *American way* is in jeopardy, they can get enough of these, "average joes" to do their bidding. Coming out armed and ready to "serve their country".

Since customs (the way we do things) have played such an important role in keeping things the way they are in America, you can expect to hear the phrase, "That's not customary", anytime someone else expresses a desire for change. *Customary* is a big part of the American vocabulary. As a Black person, I'm tired of looking around and seeing so many "customary" reminders of slavery.

I believe that there is something seriously wrong with anyone who would even *want* to harbor positive sentiments in favor of slavery. So, for someone to want to preserve the statues and marketplaces around the country, landmarks where slavery took place, is just plain evil. And has no place in the type of country that America *claims* to be.

But then, who America claims to be, and who she really is, are two different Americas. One real and one a fantasy. Many people, on both sides of the coin, cannot accept the responsibility of dealing with America's race problem. Believing that if we just ignore it, it will disappear. Talking about it, they believe, is feeding the flame. When the reality is that the flames of racism, among other flames, have been fanned since this country's inception, *having never gone out. And not talking about it*, is only compounding the problem.

CHAPTER 12

The Evolution of Media

The very first newspapers originated in America around the early part of the 18th century, as a political tool for the American Revolution. That was the modest beginnings of the American media of today. Posters and handbills(flyers) were also ways of getting information out to the local population. Getting their start in the northeastern region of the country, newspapers soon spread to whatever parts of America the European settlers claimed as their own. A newspaper was a way of keeping in touch with what was going on in various areas of the country, without having to be there. Printing presses where the newspapers were typeset and printed, were well maintained and protected.

Article Written By Lee Grayson:

"Early journalists relied on collecting information through government and private mail or messenger service, and mail service used steamships and trains to transport story information. The speed of the material arriving from the American far west increased from 1860 to 1861 with the formation of the Pony Express, which provided service from St. Joseph, Missouri, to Sacramento, California.

Story information took 10 to 16 days to travel between the two cities using the express, depending on weather conditions and the talents of the horseback riders. Information sent by stagecoach doubled this time. By the time reporters in the eastern part of America received story details, the news was almost a month old, information from international sources needed months to arrive by train or steamship. Before the use of the telegraph, American audiences read history by the time the stories appeared in the press." *

*How Did the Invention of the Telegraph Affect Journalism? (An article by Lee Grayson@ https://classroom.synonym.com/did-invention-telegraph-affect-journalism-5341.html)

   The efficiency of newspapers improved greatly with the invention of the telegraph, by Samuel Morse ushering in the use of Morse Code. Coded language was transmitted between points connected by wires. This required putting up wires, much like the ones we see along the highways today. When trans-Atlantic wires were laid in the ocean between America and the European continent, it meant that we could now receive and transmit news between the continents.

The job of newspapers was mainly to report local, national, and worldwide news, keeping the countries and cities of the world connected to each other. They achieved this through wire networks which would transmit their own events and receive events by way of transmissions from other sources around the world, put it all together and release it to the public. There were editors to choose the most important stories and to make sure the *information* was correct and without typing errors.

The invention of completely wireless radio (except for the power source) is credited to an Italian inventor by the name of Guglielmo Marconi. This was without a doubt the beginning of the true "global community," as the world has become. The technology involved in the invention of wireless radio weighed heavily in the development of television transmissions coming after. But first, wireless radio was a new and groundbreaking discovery to be celebrated.

In this article taken from the book "Split Image: African Americans in the Mass Media", by two Howard University scholars-- Jannette Dates and William Barlow, the origins of radio are discussed.

To talk about early radio, we must first keep in mind that the industry as it existed in 1920 was quite different from today. Back then, what we call "radio" was called "wireless", and it was still in a very experimental stage. Since Marconi had demonstrated at the turn of the century that a message could be sent through the air (or the "ether" as they called it) without wires, the industry had changed. Where at first it was mainly Morse code messages to and from ships, now it had become an exciting new hobby that commanded the attention of numerous boys (and a few girls) in the 19-teens. Commercial radio did not exist yet-- there were no "disc jockeys", no beautiful studios with state of the art equipment. Everybody was an amateur, and they usually built their own ham radio sets.

The equipment didn't have to be elegant-- it just had to work, and since it was often noisy, it helped to have understanding parents who didn't object to one room of the house having radio equipment in it. Because ham radio was considered a hobby, nobody expected to make any money from it; hams just had fun sending messages to faraway places. As the technology improved, messages could be sent by voice as well as by Morse code, and some hams began to "broadcast" phonograph records to entertain their friends in other cities. An enterprising few even set up their equipment in a place where live music was being played. One early experiment of this type may have involved "The Father of the Blues", W.C. Handy. There is some evidence that a white amateur named Victor H. Laughter, who admired Handy's music, sent out a concert of it from Memphis as early as November of 1914.

The majority of the young amateurs either figured out how to build radio receivers by asking their parents, or from reading the articles in the new radio magazines like "QST" and "Radio Amateur News", or they learned about radio in school. High schools of the 19-teens had begun to catch the radio craze too, and many ham radio stations were set up as a result-- it was an incentive for students to stay after school and learn while enjoying their new hobby.

Unfortunately, since America was a segregated society in the 19-teens, it was often difficult for African Americans to participate in the excitement of early broadcasting, especially in parts of the south. I have not found much evidence that Southern black high schools were able to build radio stations for their students-- given how limited the budgets of these schools often were, radio was probably considered an un-necessary luxury item. And in some of the more racist southern cities, there was a lot more to worry about than learning radio. There were all too many white business owners and farmers who depended on the cheap labour a largely illiterate black population could provide, so they actively discouraged black children from attending school beyond the elementary grades.

Historian Neil McMillen, in his book "Dark Journey: Black Mississippians in the Age of Jim Crow", documents an era when possessing NAACP literature or newspapers that advocated equal rights could get a black person arrested, when endless restrictions were placed on black citizens who wanted to vote, when only 5% of black schools had libraries (many didn't even have heat or running water), and when for every $31 spent on educating a white child, just $6 was allocated for black education (the prevailing sentiment among too many whites was that educating black kids was a waste of time-- they didn't need an education to work in the fields...). It was also an era when the Ku Klux Klan was experiencing unprecedented growth, and every day brought news stories of lynchings. Under such precarious circumstances, it is no surprise that few southern blacks were upset about the lack of a radio club in their community!

- End of Article

By the time radio had gained its commercial stride it was also not kind to Black people, with shows that portrayed Black people as whiney and using backwards dialect, full of " yassirs" (yes sirs) and "yassims" (yes mams). And anything else to make Black people feel humiliated within themselves, and disrespected and being thought of as some poor ignorant creature by other races, listening in.

I can't help but wonder if today's lack of caring about certain things, on the part of Black people, is a sort of protection that was developed over the years. When at every turn, someone is holding up an image of you that is unfavorable, there comes the need to look away and adopt an, "I prefer not to care," attitude. Otherwise, if you take these things seriously, you might have heart attacks or strokes, which is probably the intended purpose.

In all honesty, the American media, in its many forms, has played a major role in how Black people have been perceived and treated in this country. In many ways, it (the media) has been the "great overseer." Making sure that we don't get too far away from, "the plantation." Constantly trying to remind us and everyone else, that we came to this country as slaves and now have the *nerve* to want to be *treated as equals!*

  To be fair in assessing the relationship between Black people and radio, is to admit that when it came to music, radio, reluctant at first, eventually complimented Black music in a big way. When it was finally allowed "on the air" Black music became "all the rage." Taking, not only America, but the world, by storm. But before Black artists were allowed on mainstream radio, they were being successfully (financially) imitated by White artists. Let's face it, America is a huge contradiction.

  The "powers that be" tried to keep Black people who originated the music from capitalizing on it, calling it "jungle music." All, while being completely receptive to White artists performing the very same music. Some of these artists, like Elvis, I'm told, had great admiration for Black music and the people who performed it. You can try to keep the people apart, but sooner or later they find ways to come together. With music being one of the main avenues.

  "Drive west on Sunset to the sea. Turn that jungle music down. Just until we're out of town." Lyrics by Walter Fagan & Donald Becker, from a Steely Dan song "Babylon Sisters." This is an honest description of how Black people are often perceived in America. *"We want what you do. But we don't want you." "We'll take it from here."* And the Black contributions to America which have been *literally taken*, are too numerous to count. Especially when it comes to inventions.

When conventional radio began, it not only carried news, but other forms of entertainment, as well. Radio introduced shows called, "soap operas". The "soap" moniker was because the shows were mostly sponsored by detergents or soaps. These *radio* soap operas were the forerunners for what would eventually become *television* soap operas. These shows had a lot of influence on their listeners. News was reported, but most of the real interest was geared toward the drama of soap operas.

At the time newspapers were still the main source for obtaining the news, so the newspapers' information was carefully and painstakingly protected. To assure accuracy. Radio had more freedom to improvise, as long as there was nothing vulgar or indecent. The scope of the impact which radio could have on its listeners became shockingly evident during an episode of The Orson Wells Show.

As he narrated (with sound effects) that "Martians" had landed on earth, some of the people who had tuned in believed it to be true that creatures from Mars had landed on earth and some of them were so afraid that they literally committed suicide. This tragic event signaled tremendous possibilities for radio, with people seeking ways to influence others and gain, financially, from it. As entertainment came to the forefront, in radio, news was pushed to the backburner.

With the invention of television came new opportunities and possibilities for reaching the masses. Possibilities in advertising, mind-shaping, and the ability to come into peoples' homes and be thought of as virtual "friends." Along with this familiarity came a trustiness on the part of the viewers. If television said, or did it, it must be true.

Starting off with programs for family viewing, t. v., as television was now being called, began to capture the hearts and minds of America. Especially the comedy shows which made up the bulk of television shows from the beginning.

America loves a good laugh. As it had been with radio, so it was with television, Black people were placed in humiliating roles, having no dignity whatsoever. Being the butt of jokes in everyday life was just carried over to television for all of America to witness.

Often cast as someone stealing watermelons or chickens, to the point that the stereotypes are still with us, and believed, and joked about by many people even today. Sadly, some of the people still joking about these things are African Americans. ***The Dumbing Down of ~~Black~~ America!***

One such show, the "Amos 'n Andy" radio program featured White men's voices imitating Black men, using the most degrading jargon that they could think of. After the success of the radio version of "Amos 'n Andy", television gave the show a try. A major difference was that the t. v. version cast Black actors playing the lead roles. This time there were a couple of characters who showed some dignity. But for the most part, it was the same old buffoonery.

Yet, even today, some folks, including some Black people, who fondly recall the televised version of the "Amos 'n Andy" show regard it as "entertaining", applauding the fact that the actors were at least employed and being self-supporting. I can only hope that the Blacks who accepted the show believed *no one* would think that *anyone* could be that stupid in real life. That is the only way that my mind can accept it. Being denigrated right in front of your face and accepting it as funny, is something I will *never* understand.

I've noticed that people who make fun of handicapped or special needs people are often just a minor step up from the very ones that they poke fun at. In other words, people tend to put down others in order to elevate themselves from their *own* insecurities. If they can get some laughs along the way, that's just more gratifying.

As for Black people, I think that the bait is placed in front of us as a way of trying to make us *feel* inferior. I can paint a picture of you and make you look any way I want you to look and if you never see a "true" reflection of yourself, you *might* accept my version *as the real you.*

Since the media of today has evolved in so many aspects, it's uses have also increased. A very important part of media now includes weather forecasting, which can be very helpful in planning daily schedules and trips, while avoiding disasters. Since the news comes from various mediums now it is much more readily accessible.

We now have "smart phones" which double as phones and televisions in the palms of our hands. Allowing the public to know when there is immediate danger in their area, such as escaped criminals. Traffic jams can be avoided also, if known about beforehand. With other media being accessible from the same sources. Music, movies, books, videos, internet searches and many other types of media can be enjoyed directly from a cell phone.

Most Americans, and the rest of the world, are fixated on *some* type of media, waiting for the "next big thing". And the media, in all of its various forms, is competing for the opportunity to be the one which is most accommodating to these appetites.

With that being the case, the media tends to shape the thinking of the population, *giving them* (the American public) the opinion that the media wants them to have. As each new source of media emerges, the information has become more of what someone *wants* you to think, as opposed to allowing you to form your *own* opinions.

What was once based on an honor system is now sometimes *fabricated* in order to be the most sensational. With the intent of separating you from your money. Fake news is right there among the actual news. It is often hard to tell the difference. Federal regulations governing the air waves have been relaxed to the point that they are almost non-existent.

The media in many ways, controls our everyday life. From what we watch on television, to what we do by way of the internet. From what we listen to on radio to the magazines we read. I could go on because our involvement with media is endless. I'd like to point out, though, that with the *evolution* of media, newspapers have become one of its latest casualties. Very few newspapers are in existence today in America. The reason given by most publishers is that with the emergence of the internet, where news is more readily attainable and advertising dollars reach a much larger audience, newspapers are just not profitable anymore.

In today's media the line between what is news, and what is entertainment is getting harder to define. That is primarily because the general public has an insatiable appetite for what is going on in the world around them. Be it news, entertainment, or both. There are even television shows geared towards news of what is developing in the lives of the most well-known entertainers. A type of *gossip* media.

With the invention of television came the media's ability to have even more influence on the lives of their audiences. This was when *life began to imitate art* in a major way. Since radio was only able to transmit audio, it required the listeners to use their imaginations for visualizing what they were hearing. The invention of television, however, was the total opposite of radio, leaving not much to the imagination. Filling in the blanks and leaving the audience feeling more like they are *participating* in the programs.

People began buying things that they had seen on a favorite show or a certain commercial. The more they liked a show, the more they wanted to be like the *people* on that show. This did not go un-noticed by the networks and sponsors of these shows. In fact, that was the purpose. Enticing the audiences to want to have the type of lives that their favorite stars were living. *Life imitating art*. Television set that in motion, and we (the world) have never looked back.

There were shows which increased the sales of certain types of furniture, appliances, choices of clothes, hairstyles, speech, and even cars. "Lucy wore a dress like that". "Mary Tyler Moore sleeps in a bed like this." Shows like, "Leave It to Beaver", "Ozzie And Harriet" were influential to both adults *and* children. If Rick Nelson from "Ozzie And Harriet" wore a new style of shirt that no one had seen before, boys would beg their mothers to buy them a similar one.

At Christmas time television helped the children to decide what they wanted for gifts by plastering new toys all over the screen and running the commercials so often that they couldn't possibly be overlooked. After being bombarded with enough, "Momma can I's", it was a done deal. Little Johnny was getting "Blaze" the talking horse and Little Suzie was getting the latest "Barbie" doll.

As audiences were being influenced by the weekly variety shows, the daily "soap operas" had an even stronger grip on *their* "followers". And I use the word followers literally, as soap operas took the country by storm. A vast majority of housewives during the heyday of soap operas, were glued to the television set between the hours of 11am and 3pm from Monday to Friday.

Watching shows whose content was about anything that the network felt would hold their interest. Promoting almost everything. From adultery, alcoholism, drug addiction, murder, and anything controversial to keep them coming back the next day to watch the drama unfold on a continual basis.

Not only were these "soaps" (as they were affectionately referred to) watched at home but also in beauty and barber shops, in workplaces such as offices, grocery stores, and wherever televisions were located. Men, women, grandmothers, and grandfathers and everyone in between seemed to be hooked on "soaps". The news, and what was *really* going on, began to take a backseat to the fantasy world of soaps and Hollywood dream peddling.

With names like, "All My Children", "The Edge of Night", "General Hospital", "One Life To Live", and "The Guiding Light", they covered the spectrum on subject matter. Something for everyone. At first, the Black people, if there were any, were cast as maids and chauffeurs, which was being realistic for the period. As time went on, however, Blacks were cast in positions like police detectives and even in romantic situations in order to spice things up.

In all honesty, soaps took us where life had yet to go. It was fantasy in the first degree. People accepted it because it was seeing ourselves the way we *wished* we were. At least some of us did.

Early television played a big role in the acceptance of cigarette smoking in America, by using cigarette companies to sponsor many of the shows. From seeing the commercials looking so glamourous with beautiful people, automobiles, and great scenery, many of the people watching were enticed into smoking. At the time, the dangers of having a cigarette habit hadn't been fully realized and as accepted as it is today.

Another area of success in early television was variety shows, where conversations between the hosts and their guests took place. With music, singing, stand-up comedy, animal acts, juggling acts, acrobatics, dancing or some other forms of entertainment taking place in between conversations. It was a winning situation for everyone involved. To host a show meant that you were successful in acquiring sponsors, which parleyed into a decent salary. Being seen on a popular show could also work wonders in the career of an entertainer.

To be on a top show, meant that you were tops in your field, thereby guaranteeing an increase in your "asking fee" when you performed someplace. Still, there could be a burnout factor, if you were seen too much. On the other hand, you could be considered a "nobody" without *some* television exposure. Many pageants, music award shows, election debates, sports events and other presentations would be only a fraction of what they have become, without the aid of television.

Not everyone, however, was able to take advantage of the exposure that television afforded. Nat King Cole and Sammy Davis Jr. are two prime examples of the bigotry which existed in America, at that time. Both, having been successful entertainers *before* television, tried to transfer their popularity to the television screen. Each of them, as great and well-known of entertainers as they were, found that prejudice in America runs deep.

It doesn't really matter how much your *audience* loves you, if you can't keep your *sponsors* happy. Realizing this, the bigots went after the *sponsors* of Cole and Davis, thereby destroying the shows' sources of income and the opportunity to bring people together. "If you don't stop supporting those N-words, we're going to stop buying your products or services."

And it worked. The bottom line has always been the bottom line and the bottom line is money. Causing the networks to pull 2, otherwise, very successful shows. As far as America had seemingly evolved, it wasn't ready to see Black people, *especially Black men*, in such a dignified position. Plus interacting with *White people?! As if they were equals*! That was just *too much!*

"If you guys want to play Vegas that's fine, but we can't have you showing up in our living rooms every week! Having our children thinking it's okay to fraternize with your kind." The message was clear. White Americans, *enough of them anyway*, weren't ready to include us in their journey to prosperity. And even to this day, a *serious* variety show hosted by a Black male, has yet to exist for any reasonable length of time.

As long as you're willing to act like a buffoon, you're more than welcome to do so. After all, this is being who we have been saying you are, all along.

I wasn't a buffoon when I invented the traffic light or the first blood plasma bank, and I'm not about to become one now. For *any* amount of money. Racism. It's a touchy subject but why is that so? Why should I tip around something that is bringing me grief every time I'm confronted with it, which is all the time?

This is more than *an* elephant, but a *herd* of them in the room. I'm not about to feel guilty for wanting the right to be treated fairly by a system which calls itself *democratic*. But, of course, everything in America comes with an "us" and "them" stigma attached to it. Although I'm aware of it, that doesn't mean I will let my life be dictated by that double standard, because I won't.

Magazines

Magazines are a form of media whose origin is preceded only by newspapers in America.

History of Magazines in America

The first American magazines were published in 1741. Philadelphia printers Andrew Bradford and Benjamin Franklin—who owned rivaling newspapers—both raced to publish the first American magazine. Bradford ultimately claimed the honor by publishing American Magazine first. Benjamin Franklin's General Magazine was published three days later. Neither magazine met with much success: Bradford's publication folded after three months, and Franklin's lasted only six months.

Despite these short-lived ventures, magazines became incredibly popular in America. By the end of the 18th century, there were more than 100 magazines in the United States. Some of the most influential early American magazines were the Pennsylvania Magazine, which was edited by Thomas Paine, and the Massachusetts Magazine.

Early periodicals were so expensive that only the wealthy could afford them. As a result, early publications were geared toward the most learned, cultured and sophisticated individuals of the day. By the 1830s, however, less expensive magazines aimed at the general public began to emerge. Rather than maintaining the intellectual air of their predecessors, these magazines focused on amusement and entertainment.

*From an article in magazines.com, author and date unknown

https://www.magazines.com/history-of-magazines#targetText=History%20of%20Magazines%20in%20America,publish%20the%20first%20American%20magazine.&targetText=By%20the%201830s%2C%20however%2C%20less,general%20public%20began%20to%20emerge.

   Magazines have become such a part of American culture that it's hard to imagine life without them. They fill so many purposes that they can be found everywhere. In doctor's offices, at the check-out counters in department stores and grocery stores, at airports, etc. There is a magazine that represents about every facet of American life that you can think of. Many of them have been in publication longer than some existing newspapers. Whatever your pleasure, there is a magazine that covers it.

If the truth be known, magazines are a large part of the reason that America is not more of an illiterate society than it is. Because we live in such a "hurry up" world, magazines, which can be read or thumbed through quickly, have become the choice for many peoples' reading materials.

Some people who just don't have the time, but would love to spend more time reading, choose to satisfy themselves with their favorite magazines. Getting called into the doctor's office and being interrupted while reading an article, can sometimes prompt us to go and purchase the magazine to be able to finish the article.

Magazines are geared toward holding our short-term interest. The magazines that succeed are directed straight toward subject matter that is close to the hearts, or sentiments, of a particular audience. If it's sports, it's usually not just sports in general, but a specific sport. Maybe someone has an interest in wildlife. Would that be hunting, camping, or bird watching? There's a magazine, probably more than one, for each of them.

After years of being left out of mainstream (White) magazines and newspapers, Black people in America began to establish their own publications. They began to write about and report on things of interest in the Black communities across the country.

This was some time after slavery when Blacks had begun to be allowed to get jobs and start to prosper, somewhat. Right away came the criticism that this wasn't necessary. Why do they want to have separate publications from everyone else? To the Black community the answer was obvious. We were tired of being *left out*.

Black-owned companies had started to develop products that served the needs of Black people. Hair and skin products and other things that paralleled whatever the White community was doing. There were straightening combs for pressing out "kinky" hair. Cream that bleached the skin. You get the picture. Yet there were always that group of Black people who refused to emulate and imitate White people.

Companies producing Black products, naturally began to partner with the Black publications. Together they learned the importance of sponsorship and ways of protecting and encouraging each other. They developed loyal customers by being consistent and learning to follow the needs of the people closely. The magazines tended to carry news, fashion, politics, and whatever else interested the Black community, all rolled into one.

At the forefront were *Jet Magazine* and *Ebony* published by ***Johnson Publishing***, not to be confused with ***Johnson & Johnson Products***, a White company. With lynchings of Black people being very much a factor in our everyday life, *Jet Magazine*, a weekly publication, became a guardian of sorts. We looked forward to reading the latest developments of things, good and bad, happening to our people in various parts of the country. We sometimes planned our goings and comings by reading *Jet*.

If a lynching just took place in a certain location, we knew that tensions would be high in that area and would try to avoid it. One such lynching, the murder of Emmett Till, was written about in *Jet*, as a warning to Black men and boys, not to get too close to White women or the same could happen to them.

He was taken, by force, out of his cousins' home in Money, Mississippi, in the middle of the night, and brutally murdered. The assumed offense was, "Wolf-whistling" at a White store clerk in that town. A story that she recanted shortly before her recent passing, as an elderly woman. It was news that young Black men needed to know, and older Black men were all too aware of. As a courtesy and a reminder, the story of Emmett Till's death was reported in *Jet*, atleast once every year, for many years.

The significance of Emmitt's death being told by a Black publication was that *Jet* didn't hold back on showing the brutality of the crime. Working very closely with his mother in Chicago, where he resided, *Jet*, which was *also* located in Chicago, took a special interest in the story. His mother, Mrs. Mamie Till Bradley gave them permission to print a picture showing how his murderers put a hole right through the 14 year old's skull. Not allowing the morticians to cover it up, so the whole world could see, "What they did to my son."

Ebony Magazine was more of a society publication, reporting on the social aspects of Black life in America. Keeping us up on what was happening with our Black politicians. The latest fashion trends, which especially interested the ladies. Enlightening us on the lifestyles of our favorite movie stars and entertainers. General societal information concerning African Americans.

An *Ebony Magazine* on a coffee table was a symbol of Black pride and awareness. If you were a Black celebrity, having your picture on the cover of *Ebony Magazine* solidified your status in the Black community.

Of course, Black people read other publications besides the ones geared toward the African American community. The same as some White people read *Jet* and *Ebony*, when the opportunity arose, of course. They weren't likely to just walk up to a newsstand and ask for a *Jet* or *Ebony* magazine. But if a maid or co-worker left one laying around, well that's different. If we don't *snoop* on each other, how will we be able to copy the "good stuff" from each other.

There were also magazines like Sepia and Tan which catered to another area of interest. Containing articles of stories that could be comparable to soap operas, with some true crime stories thrown in. Also including some romance stories and some pictures that bordered on soft porn. These magazines were of a cheaper quality, manufacturing-wise, but most people who bought magazines were reluctant to throw them away.

Many people still find it hard to throw away their favorite magazines. When it comes time to part with them, they prefer to *give* them away, rather than *throw* them away. This is the affinity that develops between people and their reading materials. Magazines from times gone by, can be valuable commodities for their ability to denote what life was like in a certain era. They can have a nostalgic value.

Magazines have probably influenced lifestyles in America in a way that rivals television. And that is saying a lot. For instance, when Hugh Hefner decided to start publishing interesting interviews and non-porn related articles in *Playboy Magazine*, it legitimized the magazine to the point of acceptance by a much wider audience. Now its readers could claim to be indulging in the literary aspect of the magazine.

The acceptance of Playboy and other similar magazines paved the way to the eventual acceptance of pornography into mainstream America. America still, in many ways, has Puritanical values, but only when she can't find a legitimate excuse *not* to have them. "Give me a good enough reason and I will abandon that side of my morals without feeling the least bit guilty." That's *America* speaking now, not me.

If not for the publicity received from magazines like Rolling Stone, Billboard, and a slew of teen magazines, a lot of the big names in entertainment might not have achieved the stardom that they did. Rolling Stone featured some great articles, giving insight into the lives of people like Jimi Hendrix, Janis Joplin, The Beatles, Elvis and many others.

Both Billboard and Rolling Stone carried a wealth of information on the entertainment industry and the people who make it happen. You could learn something about most facets of the industry, and the industry people, by reading these publications.

Teen magazines turned their attention toward young White teens, specifically female. For the purpose of promoting the careers of their teen crushes and the young female stars that they admired and wanted to be like.

With names like *Teen* and *Sixteen*, there was no doubt about what audience they were aiming for. Young, mostly White, and with money to spend. Inserting pullout posters of their favorites for putting up on their bedroom walls and inviting them to join the fan club of their favorites was great advertising and it worked very well. I wonder if some of the record companies didn't own the magazines also.

This idea also caught on in the Black community. Magazines like *Right On!* and *Black Beat* became popular among Black teens. *Right On* containing posters of their favorite artists just like the White teen magazines. Meet and greets between the artists and the fans took place at the local record shops when the artists came to town. A picture taken with your favorite artist was a very big deal.

Then *Vibe Magazine*, with Quincey Jones at the helm, upped the ante by having crossover appeal, bringing them together under one magazine, so to speak. It was a little larger than magazines of its kind. If there even *was* another magazine like it. The layout and artwork were classier than its predecessors. The stories were more indepth, with great interviewers. *Vibe* reigned in the number one spot for quite some time. Incorporating Hip Hop and R & B. It was the magazine to be seen in.

As, Hip Hop music began to dominate, so did Hip Hop culture. Needing magazines that represented their style, a number of them appeared. In fact, the number of magazines representing the Hip Hop genre were the most ever, for one style of music. Magazines like *XXL, Hip Hop Weekly, The Source,* and *Word Up* to name a few.

Hip Hop was about to take over the world, and not just music-wise, but the whole Hip Hop culture was arriving. And to this day, it has the most dominate presence of any other music presently on the market. It has become, arguably, one of Black America's most original musical contributions to the American cultural scene.

With the advent of the computer, the media is now open to all kinds of possibilities. *Good and bad.* The World Wide Web organization has painstaking loaded the internet with almost any information that you can think to research. I say *almost*, but in fact, I have yet to search the internet and not find something to do with the object of my search. Until I encounter a problem searching for something, I will say that you can find *anything* with an internet search.

Internet can be an asset to students who must research various topics, putting books, articles, newspapers (the ones that still exist), magazines and any reading material that they might require, right at their fingertips. That is because as soon as something is written and published, it is immediately, almost magically uploaded to the internet. Someone actually is loading it, so it's not really magical, but so quick that it seems so.

You can find addresses, pay bills, check news and weather (local or elsewhere), use social media (Facebook, Twitter, etc.). All of this and much more. It's hard to talk about the internet and only mention its positive uses, because that would be misleading. There is also a murky side to the internet. Where its usage, by certain individuals, becomes sinister.

Just like the world we live in has some unsavory people living among us, so goes life in the cyber world. The same as in the real world, in order to stop them, they must be caught, first. Although the internet is a *virtual* world, it is used by *actual* criminals. They come to the internet for different reasons. Some are pedophiles looking for young victims, while pretending to be children or teenagers themselves.

Others are looking for people to take advantage of in any way that they can. Sexually, financially, romantically, and even just to spread malicious viruses to total strangers. There have been serial killers and mass murderers who have researched their evil beforehand, using the internet. And, fortunately, many have been caught the same way. Leaving a cyber trail for the authorities to follow.

In a matter of little more than one hundred years, we have gone from the discovery of wireless radio, all the way to wireless internet. During this time America has changed tremendously in many ways but our race problems seem to have *regressed* in some ways. Black people are still not accepted as full citizens.

Although people who don't feel that way about African Americans are always trying to smooth things over, Jim Crow still raises his ugly head. "Why did you bring *them* here?" "I don't care what the law says." "He's not *welcome* here." "Go back to where you came from." These are phrases that we either learn to ignore or prepare to fight or argue about, at a moment's notice.

Another weapon that is employed is, "the look." When you receive it, you know you've been served. What is most chilling is to receive "the look," from a child. There is something very sad and disturbing about seeing a *child* with that much hatred in their heart. Then you realize. This is America.

CHAPTER 13

The President

Slavery has played a constant part in America's history from its beginning up to now. It has left a lingering effect on almost everything that takes place in this country. The main reason is because some people, mainly some White southerners refuse to accept that it is over, still seeing Black Americans as aliens, with no rights in "their" country. Viewing slavery as their "noble" past. Feeling that northern "meddlers", being jealous of them, came and took away that nobility. Which is to say that they must still believe that Black people are not people at all, but just commodities.

That's the only way to justify slavery. In order to convince themselves of that, they must have had blinders on and been closed minded to all of the contributions, *besides the free labor of slavery*, which Black people have given to this country, during *and* since slavery. There is a war still being waged by many southern Whites against the northern "Yankees", whom they believe deprived them of their future by fighting, *and winning* the war, to *end* slavery.

America is a living, walking, breathing contradiction. It contradicts itself in so many ways. After the emancipation of slaves, came a time in America called the Reconstruction Era. The Thirteenth Amendment had given the slaves their freedom. The Fourteenth Amendment stated that anyone born or naturalized in America had rights as citizens. With citizenship came the right to vote. The Fifteenth Amendment forbids anyone from being denied the right to vote based on race or color.

When the UNITED STATES of AMERICA elected a Black man to the office of President (the highest office in the land) it answered *some* questions but left many more to be pondered. Seeing how everything in America is based on race, the most important question answered would have to be, "Will a Black man ever *be* president of The United States of America?"

The answer is yes. The American people elected Barak Obama, a Black man, as its 44th president. The next most probable question would be, "Will he survive a full term?" The answer to that question is also yes. Elected to, not one but 2 terms. The answer to the next question, "How will he be received?", is the one that *really* tells the story of how complex and diverse American thinking is.

This question does not have a *simple* answer, because there was *such a complexity* to the way America's first Black president was received by the nation. In some circles, he was loved, in others he was hated. Even some Black people feared him out of ignorance. By that I mean, after having been accustomed to being led by White politicians for so long, they believed that a Black man couldn't handle the job and would just, "get us in trouble." *Ignorance in the first degree.*

One prominent figure from the Black community even suggested that living under the presidency of President Obama was worse than living in slavery. I would love to hear how he arrived upon this thinking, but to date, and wisely so, he has never offered to explain the reasoning behind this thinking. *And I don't blame him.* In my mind just that statement alone diminished the important accomplishments he had achieved in the past. And sounded like the words of one who would be happier as a slave.

During President Obama's two full terms in office, he regained respect and trust for America among the other leaders of the free world. Mostly because of not being a warmonger, but a peacemaker. Also, by being someone whose word they could trust. Although this is vehemently denied by many who refuse to accept the fact that it is true, mostly because he is a Black man, *and, after all, this is America.*

After President Obama left office, the number of phony news outlets and lies from some so-called mainstream networks increased immensely, in an effort to discredit almost all of the good that he had done.

Being the offspring of the very union that a lot of Americans, White *and* Black, have trouble even envisioning. Marriage between a Black man and a White woman brought out the highest levels of racism. And from every corner of the country. Even the president's fellow politicians displayed a level of racism on a scale that was not seen in this country since the "Jim Crow" era. The president had a way of pretty much ignoring even the most blatant acts of racism during his stay in office. I believe that we can attribute this to the fact that he isn't held to the loyalty of one race over another, but being biracial himself, was impartial to all races.

President Obama, just by being himself, brought out feelings among Americans that were *very* extreme. They either loved him or hated him. But he got the job done. The opposition party to his own Democratic party, the Republican party, vowed to block him in everything that he attempted to do. And they tried to make good on that promise.

The one thing that he was most passionate about was affordable health care. He knew, as did presidents before him, that poor Americans needed health care just like the wealthy ones.

People who already *had* health care, raised the loudest voice against it. Claiming that it would drive up *their* costs and that *they* would wind up taking care of the poor. But after a long hard fight, he succeeded in delivering the Affordable Care Act. Which his political enemies quickly labeled "Obama Care", in an attempt to defame it. Little did they know, that only served to make it even *more* memorable. *And* with a Black man's name on it.

Proving the "crabs in a bucket" theory to be true, it wasn't hard to find, even some prominent members of the Black community, who were more than willing to speak against our first Black president. Some even claimed Bill Clinton as our "first Black president" simply because he sometimes hung around Black people. I suppose they were unaware that President Clinton was behind the "Three Strikes Law" which incarcerates a huge number of Black people. Many of them, for the rest of their lives. The way this law is set up, an offender could lose their freedom, after the third "strike" for just stealing a loaf of bread.

The most important thing that President Obama's election proved was that America is not exactly what it *seems* to be. America, on the surface appears to be a place that would never elect a Black man for president. However, out of all the countries, of the world, that do not have a Black majority, America is the first, *and only*, country to elect a Black man for president.

This means there's hope. But his presidency has also brought about a backlash that has stirred overt racism in America to a level which has not been seen since the civil rights era.

There is an intensity level presently operating in this country which has the potential to become very explosive. And some Americans, politicians included, are milking it for whatever they can to help further their personal agenda. At the present time, a congressional investigation is being conducted to determine whether, or not, a foreign country, namely Russia, has interfered with the elections which gave us Donald Trump, our current president. The accusation is that the Russians waged a smear campaign against his opponent, Senator Hillary Clinton, wife of former president, Bill Clinton, in order to help him win.

If found to be credible, that they did it with the knowledge and participation of Mr. Trump, a trial to determine whether or not he committed treason is sure to follow. Either way things might happen to go, it is probably going to split the country's loyalties even more deeply. People who love President Trump have vowed to stick with him, no matter what. Even when his opponents point to things that he has done, and said, which seem contrary to things which are considered "presidential."

On the other hand, his detractors claim that his followers are intent on maintaining the "status quo" in America with a, thinly veiled, policy of White supremacy. They point to the president's favorite slogan, "Make America Great Again", as a cry to take back America. From whom? A Black president, which made Blacks feel "too uppity" and empowered, is the general thinking.

To be completely honest, with my personal experiences and the things that I have seen, and lived, as a Black American, I, unlike Doctor Martin Luther King, never dreamed it possible for a Black man to be elected as president in this country. This being the country with the most recent history of outright slavery in the world.

If you want to slander a Black person in America, questioning their right to citizenship is a perfect place to start. Our right to citizenship has been questioned since our arrival in America. As an early staple of the Trump campaign, he began to publicly question President Obama's citizenship, claiming that he was born outside of American borders. When, in fact, he was born in the *state* of Hawaii.

This began a rally cry known as "birtherism". Which even *sounds* stupid. Prove your citizenship by providing a birth certificate as proof. This had never been done, or asked, of any other president to date. A blatant show of racism, which appealed to the racist element of Americans, who picked up the rally cry, "Yeah, show us your birth certificate."

Then there was the accusation that President Obama was actually of the Islamic faith and not of the Christian faith, which in America is another of the things feared to be a threat to American democracy. When it was revealed that he was of the Christian faith, they tried to blame him for a sermon given by his long time Pastor, which condemned America for its racist history. Past and present.

When that didn't work, they began to attack his family. By way of cartoons, caricatures, mems, the media, in house cruel jokes. Even accusing his wife, the stunningly beautiful mother of his two lovely daughters, of being a man.

America has no shame when it comes to the way racism has been and *is being* directed towards its African American citizens. *Regardless of status*. It feels no need to change unless it is reluctantly forced to. Either by way of protests, acts of violence (such as riots and showing of unrest) that threaten to disrupt the lives of our citizens.

From what I have seen, I don't expect much to change anytime soon. A Black person can meet every demand placed before them and it will still never be enough to satisfy the racists in this country. Simply because it is not *about* being satisfied, it's about, "I hate you and I always will." For that reason, I am not going around looking for, or expecting acceptance from anyone. I intend to be the best that I can be, by working as hard as I can. If that's not good enough then, "Oh well." I have spent way too much of my life, trying to please others, with no success. Now it's time to satisfy me.

After the 911 terrorist attack, Osama Bin Laden became America's number one enemy. And it stayed that way until, under the direction of President Obama, Bin Laden was captured and killed. Then, suddenly it wasn't such a big deal anymore. Only because the "Black" president got it done. No celebrations and very little acknowledgement for such an accomplishment.

Sometimes it feels as if this American system puts its Black citizens in the same *category* as Bin Laden, with no apparent justification, that anyone can see. We're hated and not trusted, *"just because"*, but *"without just cause."* While the whole world is watching. But then again, most Black people throughout the rest of the world aren't treated much better.

I personally believe that there was a message being sent by the politicians, who tried to block everything which President Obama tried to do. And that message is: "This is the type of opposition you will get if you ever vote for an African American for president again. We will prevent them from getting anything done. So, you just wasted your vote."

Thankfully President Barack Obama is *one* of the smartest, if not *the* smartest, president ever! Thank you, Brother. For being a friend to many. You made a lot of us proud and hopeful. And not just Black folks either. You can see it when they come to you everywhere you go, around the world. Much honor has been bestowed upon you. And you wear it well. Whether you know it or not you were *President of the World*. I think you know it. I think we *all* do!

CHAPTER 14

Why I *Hate* Black History Month

I have come to hate the term, "Black History Month". I consider it an affront to Black people. It has a way of *excluding* us from history, at large, while *pretending to be generous*. It is a type of "affirmative action". "Okay we left you and your contributions out of the history books but allow us to make up for it. Here. Take a month, the shortest month of the year and do your thing.

Can't have this Black stuff carrying on for too long or others will get jealous. After all, there is no, White history, Native history, Asian history, Hispanic history. Get the picture? What makes you guys so special that you have to have your *own* history anyway? We will help you out by running a few documentaries about slavery and we'll definitely show some films on Dr. King."

Wait! Let's get something straight. There is no *such thing* as "Black History". There is just history. Period! With everyone participating in whatever way they did. Be it good, bad, or indifferent. It's *all history* and the only thing that differentiates history is *time*. No one has the right to dictate history by including or excluding the facts. That's what *makes it history*. It happened.

If you want to use the word, "Black", in a historical context it would be, "The history of Black people". Which would begin as far back as anyone could trace the origin of Black people. I believe that would place us somewhere in Africa. And to do it properly would be to include everything attributed to Black people from the beginning until the present time.

Terming Black peoples' time in America as just, *"Black history"*, is limiting us and not painting the whole picture. We are as historically inclusive to America, in the way of contributions, as any other race in this country. We are inventers, chemists, statesmen, entrepreneurs. But *American* history, as contained in the history books doesn't reflect that.

The history of Black people in America should have been kept by the same White historians who noted the *rest* of America's history. And should be in *all* of the history books. We were *kept out* as a way of hiding our true, and lengthy contributions to the evolution of this country. Leaving us out of the history books, except to mention that we were slaves, leaves us with only a knowledge of our history of slavery and our present state, which is not the whole truth and leaves much to be desired in the way of instilling racial pride. It is what is called, "lying by omission." Leaving things out as if they never happened.

That is why we must move on from spending so much time thinking and talking about slavery, and dig deeper into our *complete history,* with the intent of establishing a sense of pride and understanding of who we *really* are. We know that *slavery happened to us* and now it's time to stop complaining about it and get past it. In my opinion, *slavery has served to make us stronger, not weaker.* We came *through it and survived it!* That is proof that we are a strong people. You would think that most people would rather see Black people as contributors to something more than the detriment of this country. But the present general perception of Black people serves the purpose of alienating us from other races, which only aids the cause of those who seek to oppress us.

If *everyone* sees us as non-contributors, then that is a deep hole to climb out of. But sadly, since that has been the perception of us for so long, some people of other races have accepted it as who we are and seem to *even want* that to be Black peoples' station in life. "Oh, you're just Black. You can't be serious about wanting to live like the rest of us. Get back where you belong!"

This presents a serious need for bringing our past accomplishments in this country, to the forefront. So not only will *others* know, but, most importantly, *to begin to instill pride and purpose in our own young ones.*

As we see that we have been left out of the history books, we know that we can't expect any help from the so-called "Historians". That is why we must undertake the job ourselves. Not knowing how to handle our new-found freedom after emancipation, and after the passage of the Civil Rights Bill, has cost us dearly in the way of progress.

But *neither* of these landmark decisions in our history have been without real opposition from the establishment. So, in that respect, it's not completely the fault of Black people. However, it is time that we took responsibility for *our part* in the matter.

It's foolish to expect someone who has proven not to have your best interest at heart to begin to suddenly change. As a people, we must learn to promote and preserve our own part of history. And that's what it is, a *part* of history. *Not a separate history. Our history* was created *along with everyone else's history* in this country from the past until now.

Because slavery has been such a profound part of our history and brought us such misery, we tend to blame it for *all* of our ills. Knowing full well that many of our afflictions are *self-inflicted*. Caused by our unwillingness to break out from under the cloud of inferiority. Some of us believing that we *can't* do any better.

If we are going to overcome the obstacles, we need to *work* at least *twice* as hard as we *complain*.

I complain as loudly as anyone about the treatment of Black people, by police, but in all honesty, I have to wonder if the habitual criminality on the part of some Black offenders doesn't invite the habitual and systematic police brutality on the part of the police. Some Black people believe that *all* police officers are anti Black and some police believe that all Black people are anti-police. Each of us has some work to do.

There is a saying, "If you don't know where you came from; you won't know where you're going". This is very true. Reflection can be a good thing if it helps you to move forward. This is more necessary on the part of Black people than anyone else in this country, except the Native peoples. We need to search out our contributions to America, if for no other reason than to feel better about ourselves and increase our own self-esteem.

It would be great for people who are not Black to know that we are not, as a race, what we have been purported to be. Of course, some people already have the mindset that we are bad news and won't see it any differently, but some others might be willing to accept the truth.

Sometimes when sitting at a stoplight, I reflect on the fact that it was invented by a Black man. It leaves me feeling proud, yet inadequate. Proud that such a relevant contribution to modern history was made by a Black man. The feeling of inadequacy comes from not having done as much *as I can* to make *my own* contribution to society. Which is also a good thing because it leaves me with a sense of inspiration and an urgency to do something.

Just think. If even half of the people in the United States realized that the traffic light was invented by a Black man (Garrett Morgan) many of them would see Black Americans in a different light.

But then, that is the problem. There is a system at work in America, which feels there is a danger in having Black people looked upon favorably by those outside of their own race or even *those of their own race*. If that began to happen, the stereotypes which have been strategically cultivated over time, to keep us "in our place", might not be taken seriously anymore.

There is an imaginary perimeter that has been placed around African Americans to keep them mistrusted, misunderstood, misrepresented, and misguided for the purpose of alienating us from the other races. In order that none of us (the races) should join forces to fight against a system which is keeping *all of us* where they want us.

We're just the scapegoat that they pin the bad things on, to preoccupy the others with watching and possibly fearing us, *while they deceive us all.*

I am dedicating this chapter to educating myself and you, the readers, about some of the many contributions which Black men and women have made to enhance the lives of the people of this great nation. We will begin with the following list of rules to live by. Written by Dr. George Washington Carver who was much more than just "The Peanut Man."

Eight Cardinal Virtues Compiled by George Washington Carver

- Be clean both inside and out.
- Neither look up to the rich nor down on the poor.
- Lose, if need be, without squealing.
- Win without bragging.
- Always be considerate of women, children, and older people.
- Be too brave to lie.
- Be too generous to cheat.
- Take your share of the world and let others take theirs

Taken from: History Archived June 7, 2012, at the Wayback Machine from the Carver Academy website

African American Inventors

Dr. Carver, who was famous for his discovery of the many uses of peanuts, also, through his lab research, discovered and passed on to the American farmers that planting the same crop every year would deplete the soil of its nutrients. He suggested rotating crops yearly, the farmers took heed and are using that technique still. It was purported to be a rumor that, as a child, Dr. Carver was castrated by his owner, Moses Carver, in order to be trusted around White women. After his death the medical examiner is said to have confirmed that where Dr. Carvers testicles would have been, there was only scar tissue. Leading him to believe that at some point in his life, he had indeed, been castrated.

Jan Ernst Matzeliger invented the shoe last machine which connected the upper part of the shoe to the sole of the shoe. Up until the time of his invention, this work was done by skilled laborers, who held the industry hostage, in a way. Because these shoe lasters were so well paid, it caused shoes to be very expensive. Working exhaustively, without food or rest for long periods of time, he completed his invention revolutionizing the shoe industry. He never got to reap the benefits, dying an early death from tuberculosis brought on by exhaustion.

An excerpt from: Wikipedia
https://en.wikipedia.org/wiki/Jan_Ernst_Matzeliger#cite_note-4

Which citied these sources(1) 'Now Everyone Can Afford Decent Shoes'. Archived from the original on August 21, 2012. Retrieved December 5, 2012.

(2) "Jan Ernst Matzeliger "Lasting Machine". *Lemelson-MIT*. Massachusetts Institute of Technology. Retrieved 29 February 2016

Matzeliger's invention was perhaps "the most important invention for New England." His invention was "the greatest forward step in the shoe industry," according to the church bulletin of The Church of Christ (the same church that took him as a member) as part of a commemoration held in 1967 in his honor. Yet, because of the color of his skin, he was not mentioned in the history books until recently.

Garrett Morgan invented the first gas mask.

From Wikipedia: Sources cited are

(1) Inventor of the Week: Garrett A. Morgan: The Safety Hood, MIT, February 1997. Archived April 15, 2004, at the Wayback Machine
(2) Who Made America? Pioneers: Garrett Augustus Morgan PBS.org.
(3) Sisson, Mary (2008). "Garrett Morgan". In Cavendish, Marshall (ed.). *Inventors and Inventions*. Volume 4. pp. 1101–1107. ISBN 978-0-7614-7767-9.
Retrieved October 1, 2013. Later designs would include an air bag containing about 15 minutes' worth of fresh air.

Garrett Morgan invented a safety hood smoke protection device after seeing firefighters struggling from the smoke they encountered in the line of duty.[4] His device used a wet sponge to filter out smoke and cool the air.[12] It also took advantage of the way smoke and fumes tend to rise to higher positions while leaving a layer of more breathable air below, by using an air intake tube that dangled near the floor.[9] The safety hood used a series of tubes to draw clean air off the lowest level the tubes could extend to. Smoke, being hotter than the air around it, rises, and by drawing air from the ground, the Safety Hood provided the user with a way to perform emergency respiration.

- As stated previously Garrett Morgan also invented the first traffic signal as we know it today.
- Benjamin Banneker invented America's first clock
- George T. Sampson invented the first clothes dryer
- John Purdy invented folding chairs
- Alice H. Parker invented the gas heating furnace
- Marie Van Brittan Brown invented the home security system
- Sarah Boone invented the ironing board
- Thomas Elkins invented the modern toilet
- Thomas W. Stewart invented the mop
- Otis Boykin invented the pacemaker
- John Lee Love invented the portable pencil sharpener
- William Richardson invented the reversable baby stroller
- Frederick Jones invented the thermostat and temperature control
- Dr. Shirley Ann Jackson invented the touch-tone telephone, she gave us the portable fax machine, caller ID, call waiting, and the fiber-optic cable.

Although these are *only a few* of the inventions attributed to Black people, how can anyone say that they are not creditable enough to be listed in the so-called history books. And let me say that, although I dislike the fact that our "so-called" Black History has been put into a *neat little box*, called "Black History Month", it's necessary to keep it going until we are a part of the history lessons taught from a *real* history book. With the *completeness* of who we are and *all* of our contributions.

African American Politicians

Here is a list of some notable African American Politicians:

- Adam Clayton Powell Jr. (Congressman)
- Hiram Rhodes Revels (Senator)
- Edward Brooke (Senator)
- Frederick Douglass (Statesman)
- Shirley Chisholm (Congresswoman)
- Barbara Jordan (Senator)
- Barack Obama (President & Senator) *
- Elijah Cummings (Congressman)
- Maxine Waters (Congresswoman)
- Joseph Rainey (Congressman)
- Jim Clyburn (Congressman)
- Sheila Jackson Lee (Congresswoman)
- John Lewis (Congressman)
- Eric Holder (Attorney General)
- Jesse Jackson (Political Activist)
- Colin Powell (Secretary of State)
- Condoleezza Rice (Secretary of State)
- Thurgood Marshall (Supreme Court Justice)
- Julian Bond (Political Activist)
- Harold Washington (Mayor)
- John Conyers (Congressman)
- Robert Smalls (Congressman)
- Robert C. De Large (House of Representatives)
- Andrew Young (U.S. Ambassador to the United Nations)

* First and only African American President

321
African American Writers

Here is a list of some notable African American Writers:

- W.E.B Dubois
- James Baldwin
- Maya Angelou
- Langston Hughes
- Alice Walker
- Richard Wright
- Paul Laurence Dunbar
- Lorraine Hansberry
- Gwendolyn Brooks
- Amiri Baraka
- Walter Mosley
- Booker T. Washington
- Nikki Giovanni
- Phillis Wheatley
- Alex Haley
- Chester Himes
- Henry Louis Gates Jr.
- Claude McKay
- James Weldon Johnson
- August Wilson
- Martin Luther King Jr.
- Toni Cade Bambara
- Charles Waddell Chesnutt
- Toni Morrison
- bell hooks

African American Scientists

Here is a list of some notable African American Scientists:

- Marie Taylor (Botanist)
- George Washington Carver (Scientist)
- Marie Maynard Daly (Biochemist)
- Ernest Everett Just (Biologist)
- Ronald McNair (Astronaut)
- Edward Bouchet (Physicist)
- Alice Ball (Chemist)
- Emmett Chappelle (Scientist)
- Lloyd Hall (Chemist)
- Roger Arliner Young (Scientist)
- Jewel Plummer Cobb (Biologist)
- Herman Branson (Physicist)
- J. Ernest Wilkins Jr. (Scientist)
- Margaret S. Collins (Entomologist)
- Joan Murrell Owens (Biologist)
- Mae C. Jemison (Astronaut/Engineer)
- Katherine Johnson (Mathematician)*

Further research of these names will reveal the spectacular contributions that they have made to American Science.

*Her orbital mechanics calculations were necessary to the success of America's own first spaceflight, and the ones which followed.

CHAPTER 15

A Farewell to Welfare

The debate concerning welfare has been raging since shortly after it was instated, until the present time. People have varying opinions concerning welfare. Many people erroneously believe that the number of African American recipients of welfare is much higher than the number of White Americans, but this is not true as discussed in an article from TIME magazine:(Welfare: A White Secret by Barbara Ehrenreich Sunday, June 24, 2001) I found the article interesting in its facts, but although written by a White author, mocking in its tone. That is, it seems to mock White people, which is my reason not for using it here.

Arguments about who benefits most from welfare can be pretty much like political arguments. In one way they *are* exactly political. The welfare debate has been political for some time now. Still, this is not about the political aspect but the social aspect.

My personal view of welfare is that it is a new form of indentured servitude, akin to slavery. Only, this time without the whips and chains but still having possession of human lives, to a certain degree. And the difference, this time around is, many of those caught up in this *new type of slavery* are White.

As long as you reach out your hand, and someone puts money into it, that makes it hard to break the cycle of servitude. And there are *quite a few* people who *hate* being on welfare, but realize that without it, they could be homeless and starving to death.

With the revised system of welfare, (implemented by President Bill Clinton) many more people are homeless and starving anyway. Having instituted a lifetime limit to the number of total years (5) that a recipient can receive benefits, welfare is no longer a safety net for many poor people. And many former recipients have had no choice but to accept low-paying jobs.

With all the rage about how the economy is booming, there is very little talk about the fact of many people having to take on two, or sometimes three, different jobs to make ends meet because of low wages.

Because of its ability to "keep people in their places", I believe welfare is a system that is loved and welcomed by those very same politicians who speak against it. They speak against it intending to make the working- class vote for them in hopes of them dismantling it. Which they promise to, but never do, because it's their "cash cow".

So, welfare winds up serving their political purposes on each election day. Maybe because of the years between elections, voters forget the past and tend to elect politicians on the same platforms which they, or some other politician promised but didn't deliver on, during the last election period.

"Vote for me and I will disband welfare. Make them lazy so and so's have to *work* for a living". How many times have we heard *that* statement? It sounds good to the working class, who are concerned that their tax dollars are going to feed and house welfare recipients. The reality is, there are so many people on the welfare system that if it were terminated today, *millions of people* would starve to death and be homeless.

Even some of those who "pulled themselves up out of the depths of poverty and welfare assistance" speak of it as if it is the most awful thing. In truth, welfare is necessary. Still yet another truth is, being on any type of assistance, can, and most often does, destroy a person's initiative to reach higher and do better. It's not like people on welfare are even *getting enough* to be prosperous. It wasn't designed that way.

In my mind, I can't help but believe that many of those who are fortunate and prosperous enough not to need welfare, enjoy the fact that they don't have to compete in the job market with those who are receiving assistance.

The United Negro College Fund uses a slogan which says. "A mind is a terrible thing to waste." I can only imagine how many brilliant minds have been left to become so much less than what their mental abilities made them capable of. All because *poverty* forced them into a dead-end existence.

The question begs to be answered, "Whose fault is that?" For the answer, you would have to be willing to accept the truth about the history of the deep seated, institutionalized racism saturating the fabric of America. I am not naïve enough to think that there are no poor Whites in America. But the fact remains that Blacks are the, "the last hired and the first fired."

Even welfare itself discriminates. Workers charged with enforcing the laws of what welfare allows, and doesn't allow, are trained to lean heavier on Black recipients than those of other races. Even though they know that the Black recipients have a much lesser chance of getting off assistance.

There is a system at work in this country that is designed to keep poor people, especially Black people, from becoming able to compete for the finer jobs, homes, schools and just wealth in general that America has to offer. There are always some exceptions to the rule. Some Black folks do break through the ranks, but without ever receiving the full membership to this "elite" club called affluence, though. Because it is, in many ways, similar to the caste system of India, whereby if you were not born into the wealthy sector of that society, you will *never* gain entrance. Not even money can *buy* you that privilege.

In America though, those Black people who do get to rub shoulders with the White elite sometimes tend to look down their noses with an, "If I did it, you can also. There are no excuses," attitude. At the same time, there are those who achieve and never forget where they come from.

The reality is that the establishment usually tries harder to destroy *these* people because they are attempting to awaken the ignorant and that type of competition is feared. The system works better *for the ruling class* by keeping the masses ignorant.

There is a place in American society for a Black person who will publicly put down his own race, because it is an inside job, with the puppet master pulling the strings from behind the scenes, without it being known that he is even involved. Too many prominent Black people are willing participants. More than happy to serve the wishes of the ones they emulate.

The Republican Party has begun a campaign to raise the numbers of its African American membership by stating that since we have been accustomed to belonging exclusively to the Democratic Party for so long, and to no avail, that we should give *them* a chance. Few politicians of *either* party have been of assistance to the Black plight. The Kennedys, John and Bobby did some meaningful things for the Black cause but were cut down in their prime and although being a friend to Blacks might not have been the *whole story*, I am convinced that it was a big part of it.

The Republican party is often accused of being the party who wants to dismantle the welfare system, but as I stated previously, a Democratic president, President Bill Clinton, is the one who revised welfare.

There is no denying that the welfare system needs to be revised and eventually dismantled but to do it without giving recipients a way out that won't leave them starving and homeless, is just plain cruel.

If it wasn't for the assistance from welfare, we might not have had these famous people to celebrate: Oprah Winfrey, Whoopie Goldberg, Taraji P. Henson, Viola Davis, and Iyanla Vanzant, whom, by their own admission, all passed through welfare assistance and turned things around.

CHAPTER 16

She Loves Me Not

I consider myself to be a *grandchild* of the African continent, without knowing what *country* in Africa my ancestors were from, I know that they were from Africa. But I am a *child* of America. An *unwanted* child. A child whose parents were raped by America and became pregnant with me. Now I am a reminder of that and am hated because of it. The rapists then put forth their best efforts to keep me uneducated. And now have the nerve to call me stupid.

When I tried to stand up, you knocked me down and you're still knocking me down. You've even come up with new and subtle laws to condone your behavior. Before, you didn't *need* laws, because you were in *complete control*. Now you're not.

The loss of any control at all has you groping for ways to regain what you've lost. But it's not possible. We won't let you. We're not going back to the way things used to be. Not ever. So, while I'm still willing to forgive, but not forget, you would be wise to indulge me in some meaningful dialogue. That would be good for both of us.

It can only be too late if *you* think that war between us is the answer. I know that you're not afraid to fight me. And I know that you know *how* to fight. You've been viciously fighting my people ever since you brought us here.

Some say we're natural enemies, but I don't believe that. If I did, I would be on the offensive myself. After all, "self-preservation is the first law of nature". *But I'm not selfish*. I want us *both* to live and prosper. In fact, the reason that I'm holding back my aggression toward you is, if I ever stop, neither of us will survive the carnage that would take place.

You are aware that *most people* in America are armed in one way or another. I'm sure *you* are. Oh, I know you've saved the very best fire power for this occasion. *And I'm not afraid*. I just think it would be stupid to destroy such a lovely country because of your hatred for me.

All this talk about making America great again is just a thinly veiled attempt at turning White America's attention to the fact that a Black man was elected to the office of president and led the nation for eight years. For him to be elected as president, some *White* voters had to break ranks and vote for him. We didn't do that by *ourselves*! That is what you're incensed about. How could you help this child of the enemy?

What enemy!? I rub shoulders with you on a daily basis. I work side by side with you. When you start wars, for whatever reason, my dumb self goes to help you fight them. Feeling patriotic. Then, I come back to a country that doesn't even respect me or my contributions to this nation.

What is wrong with you? You're steadily trying to keep me down while pretending like *I'm* doing something to *you*. You hypocrite. The way I see it, I'm more of an enemy to *myself* than I am to *you*. And I'm sure you know it because you speak on it. "Black on Black crime".

If I looked hard enough, I could find ways to blame *that* on *you*. But at this point, I'm seeking solutions. Sometimes it seems like *you* don't really *want* solutions if it means that you and I would have to co-exist in peace. You *enjoy* considering me to be your enemy. In your mind it legitimizes your hatred for me.

You lie to yourself about who I am. Lazy, shiftless, thieving, ungrateful. Let's break things down. Who is lazier than someone who steals, enslaves another race of people to do all of his work and never even apologizes or compensates them in any way? In fact, he acts as if it's their own fault somehow. Even tells them to "Go back where you came from". *The same one who stole them from there in the first place.*

Some people ask me why I don't hate you. Love is too precious to let hate dictate. I've had glimpses of hate and I don't like it. I immediately reject any feelings of hate that creep into my spirit.

On the other hand, you reject any feelings of compassion toward me, believing that it makes you weak and encourages me to want an intimate relationship with you. I'm thankful that not everyone who *looks* like you, *thinks* like you do. But *you want me to believe* that they do.

You're playing a game, which in America, is the number one game. The "numbers game." Numbers mean everything to you. "There are more of me than there are of you." That *may* be true, but thankfully, once again not all of them *think* like you do. The lies that you have spread about me being such a threat to you, are being seen through and disproven by some who care to look deeper and be fair in *their* assessment of me.

With many of the barriers that have kept us apart for so long, being revealed, they have had an opportunity to see me for who I *really* am. My humane side *and* my flaws. After all we're just people. Like you. So, while some of us are murderers, rapists, and thieves. Some of you are guilty of the same. But like you, that does not define us as a people. It's just a *part* of who we are.

And yet, while you enjoy a life that is somewhat removed from the undesirables of *your* race by escaping to suburbia, I'm left to rub shoulders with mine being forced to live in such close proximity that they can reach out and touch me at any time. I might add though, that on top of dealing with the crime and corruption in my own community, you are taking every opportunity to try to keep me down, as well. If, by some good graces, I'm able to pull myself up, I'm told to. "Get back where you belong."

You don't have to look to incoming immigrants to find * "your tired, your poor, your huddled masses yearning to breathe free." Black people in America *ARE* "Your huddled masses yearning to breathe free." And lately you've begun to tighten the chokehold making it even *harder* to breathe at all.

**Excerpt from the poem," The New Colossus", written by Emma Lazarus and placed on the base of the Statue of Liberty.*

Any book written concerning the lives and achievements of Black people in America would be remiss not to mention certain cornerstones who have been vital, each in their own way, to the forward motion of the African American population.

- Muhammed Ali
- Harriet Tubman
- Stevie Wonder
- Sojourner Truth
- Sam Cooke
- Joe Louis
- Marcus Garvey
- Paul Robeson
- Rosa Parks
- Aretha Franklin
- John H. Johnson
- Gordon Parks
- Nat King Cole
- Harry Belafonte
- Louis Armstrong
- Jackie Robinson
- Marian Anderson
- Arthur Ashe
- Althea Gibson
- Frederick Douglass
- Woody Strode
- Nat Turner
- Oprah Winfrey
- Billie "Lady Day" Holiday
- Quincey Jones

Spike Lee
Michael Jackson
Prince
Ray Charles
Duke Ellington
Hank Aaron
Doug Williams
Diahann Carroll
Sidney Poitier
Don Cornelius
Jack Johnson
James Weldon Johnson

And last, but certainly not least, I thank Minister Louis Farrakhan (Nation of Islam) for implementing "The Million Man March" which instilled pride and a sense of togetherness in Black men across America. Especially, in light of the efforts put forth by the oppressive system working so hard to try to keep us apart. Thank you, Sir.

"If you have the *will* to succeed; you *will*."

www.ingramcontent.com/pod-product-compliance
Lightning Source LLC
Chambersburg PA
CBHW022103150426
43195CB00008B/249